Making Classroom
Assessment Work

Making Classroom Assessment Work

Anne Davies

Connections
Publishing

Merville, British Columbia, Canada

© 2000 Classroom Connections International Inc.

Printed and bound in Canada by Hignell Printing Limited

05 04 03 02 01 00   5 4 3 2 1

Cover art and book design by Anthony Alexander

Canadian Cataloguing in Publication Data

Davies, Anne, 1955-

  Making classroom assessment work

  ISBN 0-9682160-4-8

  1. Educational tests and measurements. I. Title.

LB3051.D38 2000   371.26   C00-910579-4

Additional copies of this book are available from:
Connections Publishing
P.O. Box 488
Merville, British Columbia
V0R 2M0
Canada

(250) 337-5534
(800) 603-9888
(250) 337-8113 (fax)

Discounts available on bulk orders.

Contents

In memory of my Mom and my Mom-in-law

Patricia Davies
1923–1994

Blanche Duncan
1920–1999

and

In celebration of their first great-grandchildren
Kayla and Dakota

Preface

When you look at an inuksuk you are seeing the thoughts of another person left upon the land . . . just like words in a book.

Norman Hallendy
in the foreword to *The Inuksuk Book*, by Mary Wallace

Inukshuks* are markers made of stones, often stacked in the shape of a person. They are guides for travellers on the tundra—a place where few if any landmarks are available. In the Arctic, Inukshuks can make the difference between reaching a destination successfully or not getting there at all. Finding our way to making classroom assessment work for us, our students, and their learning can be a journey with few Inukshuks to guide us.

Classroom teachers, working alongside students, are learning more about what kinds of classroom assessment activities make a difference. Black and Wiliam (1998), summarizing a decade of classroom assessment research conducted internationally, conclude that involving students in assessment and increasing the amount of descriptive feedback while decreasing evaluative feedback has a more powerful positive impact on learning than any educational innovation ever documented. As teachers seeking to support student learning through classroom assessment, we want to know how best to assess and evaluate student learning. We are looking for answers.

There are many right ways to support student learning through classroom assessment. There are no hard and fast rules, only ideas to be thoughtfully explored and decisions to be made. As teachers we know that what works with one student or group of students may not work as well with another. Just as there are many right ways to teach, no one can tell you exactly how you should assess your students.

This book identifies key decision points in planning and carrying out classroom assessment that supports learning. As you think through the concepts and ideas in each chapter and make decisions about what is

* In Inuktitut: inuksuit (plural), inuksuk (singular).

important for you, your students, and their learning, you will build your own guide—your Inukshuk. It will help you know where you are going and also guide your students in their learning. Making thoughtful decisions in response to the right questions is the best way I know to get started on the journey. I wish you well.

Chapter 1

Making Classroom Assessment Work

> In the hurry of our lives and in the rush of the inflated curriculum, we need rituals and tools that invite us to pause and make meaning from the bits of our lives. In order for this to happen in classrooms, teachers and children need to listen not only to each other but also to themselves.
>
> Lucy Calkins

An important first step for making classroom assessment work is to understand the difference between assessment and evaluation. Some people use the terms *assessment* and *evaluation* interchangeably, but they have different meanings. When we assess, we are gathering information about student learning that informs our teaching and helps students learn more. We may teach differently, based on what we find as we assess. When we evaluate, we decide whether or not students have learned what they needed to learn and how well they have learned it. Evaluation is a process of reviewing the evidence and determining its value. To illustrate the difference, Caren Cameron and Tom McRae shared the following scenario, originally developed by Michael Burger:

> Three students are taking a course in how to pack a parachute. Imagine that the class average is represented by a dotted line. Student Number One initially scored very high, but his scores have dropped as the end of the course approaches. Student Number Two's evaluations are erratic. Sometimes he does very well and sometimes he doesn't. The teacher has a hard time predicting from day to day how he will do. Student Number Three did very poorly in relation to the class for the first two-thirds of the course, but has lately figured out how to successfully pack a parachute.

Which of these students would you want to pack your parachute? Number One? Number Two? Number Three? Most people would choose Number Three. The problem is that Number Three did not pass the course. When his marks were tallied and averaged, they weren't high enough. Number One and Number Two did pass.

Packing a Parachute

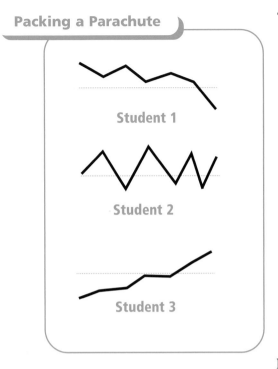

Student 1

Student 2

Student 3

Think about it. When should we assess and when should we evaluate? What might be the results of evaluating too early or too much? How do we know if we are evaluating the right things? How do we know what makes sense for the learner and for the course?

When students are acquiring new skills, knowledge, and understanding, they need a chance to practice. This is the learning process. Assessment involves learners receiving a considerable amount of descriptive feedback during their learning. Descriptive feedback gives information that enables the learner to adjust what he or she is doing in order to get better (Sutton 1997 cites Gibbs and Stobart 1993). Descriptive feedback comes from many sources. It may be specific comments about the work, information such as posted criteria that describe quality, or models and exemplars that show what quality can look like.

Evaluative feedback is different. It tells the learner how she or he has performed as compared to others or to some standard. When we evaluate, we consider the evidence and decide whether or not students have learned what they needed to learn and how well they have learned it. Evaluative feedback is often reported using letters, numbers, checks, or other symbols—it is encoded. If we evaluate too early, we limit descriptive feedback and risk interrupting the learning. When we assess during the learning and evaluate at the end of the learning, we give students time to practice and learn before we judge the evidence.

A Classroom Assessment Process That Works

There are three general parts to a classroom assessment process that works. First, teachers review the curriculum and standards documents and describe for themselves the learning that students are expected to accomplish. They collect and review samples and models that show what the learning looks like for students of a particular age range, and they think through what kinds of evidence their students could produce to show they have learned what they needed to learn.

Once the big picture is established, teachers work with students to bring them into the assessment process. They do this by talking about the learning, showing samples and discussing what the evidence might look like, setting criteria with students, and giving them time to learn.

As students participate in assessment, they learn to become partners in the continuous assessment cycle. In this cycle, students talk about what needs to be learned, set criteria, and receive and give themselves descriptive feedback. From time to time they self-assess and set goals. They debrief their learning and revisit the criteria as they learn more. They present their work to others and receive more feedback. This cycle continues as students are involved in resetting criteria and continuing their learning.

Seeing It Work

What does this process look like in a classroom? The rest of this chapter presents an example of what assessment and instruction can look like. In this example students are learning how to conduct a research project.

Talking About the Learning

> We are going to be working on a research project over the next few weeks. It is important for you to learn how to gather information and make sense of it for yourself and your life. Think about the Internet. There is a lot of information available. But for it to be of any use, you have to decide what you want to know, make choices about what information to take seriously and what to ignore, and then decide what it all means for you. That's being a critical thinker—a thoughtful user of information. So, what do you think is important about a research project?

When students are engaged in conversation before any learning activity or task, the talk clarifies options, highlights possible plans, and encourages sharing of information with others. As students work with teachers to define what learning is and what it looks like, they shift from being passive learners to being actively involved in their own learning. By being engaged, they use and build more neural pathways in their brains (Goleman 1995; Jensen 1998; Pinker 1997). This means they are more likely to be able to access their learning more easily and for a longer period of time—way beyond the end of the unit or test.

When teachers talk about what is to be learned and why it is relevant to students' lives, and invite students to define what it might look like once they've learned it, students begin to understand what needs to be learned, and they have a chance to prepare to learn. Many learning theorists propose that we interpret the world through our mental models—we see what we expect to see and hear what we expect to hear. Emerging brain research supports this perspective (Pinker 1997). When students are involved from the beginning, they are more ready to learn. When we involve students in shaping their learning, they are more likely to:

- understand what is expected of them
- access prior knowledge
- have some ownership over making it happen
- be able to give themselves descriptive feedback as they are learning
- give information teachers need to adjust their teaching

Knowing what they are learning and what it looks like gives students the information they need to assess themselves as they learn—to keep themselves on track. Learning to self-monitor in this way is an essential skill for independent, self-directed, lifelong learners.

Showing Samples and Discussing the Evidence

> I am going to give you several examples of research projects. Here is a poster, a video, a booklet, and a timeline. I want you to work in groups to analyze these student projects and think about what is really important in a research project. Especially think about how information is effectively communicated. When you are ready, we will list your ideas and create criteria for our research project. We can record the criteria on a T-chart so you can refer to it as you work.

When we give students samples to review, and when we talk with them about what is important in their learning, we help them build mental models of what success looks like. This is particularly important for the students who struggle the most.

When teachers spend time with students, sharing samples as well as connecting what students already know to what they need to know, students' understanding of what they will be learning and of what will be assessed increases. When we involve students in this way, they use their prior knowledge and learn more about the language of learning and assessment. They also begin to understand what evidence looks like and find out what is important—what *counts*.

Be careful when choosing samples to show students. If samples are limited to showing what students already know and can do, they fail to orient students towards what they need to know next. When samples represent work that is too far away from what students know and are able to do, students may not see how to get from where they are to where they need to be (Hillocks 1986).

Getting on with the Learning

> It's time for you to get started on your research projects. We are going to begin with a small research project so you can all practice with the support of a group before you do a larger research project independently. This is also a chance for you to find out what you already know about doing a research project and a chance to learn from your group members.
>
> For this first project I would like you to work in small groups. I want your group to choose something you are interested in learning more about. Choose something where the information will be easy to find, since you will only have a week to do this research project. Perhaps it will be something you already know a lot about, such as a sport, music, or pets. Think of topics that interest you and your classmates. In a week's time your group will present to the class. At that time, we will be using the criteria we created to assess your work—keep it in mind as you work.

Giving students time to discover what they already know and to learn from each other provides a scaffold for future learning. When conversations about learning take place in the group, learners can check their thinking and performance and develop deeper understanding of their learning. Researchers studying the role of emotions and the brain say that experiences such as these prepare learners to take the risks necessary for learning (Le Doux 1996; Goleman 1995).

Doing things more than once is also essential for learning. Michael Schmoker (1996) says that in education we tend to jump on one bandwagon and then jump on the next one to come along. He argues that we would learn more as a profession if we just stuck to one thing and learned how to do it well. The same is true for our students. It is when they do something the second and third time that they learn what they know and what they need to know. Students need practice time to learn. It is when students practise that they are able to take what they are learning and apply it at deeper and deeper levels.

Presenting

> Class, you've had a week to work on your research projects. Tomorrow you'll be presenting your work to the class. Please sign up with Terry and Cheryl if you want your presentation videotaped. It will be your decision whether or not to include the video in your portfolio.
>
> Remember our purpose. This was a chance for you to find out what you already knew about doing a research project as well as to learn from your group members. As I said before, we are going to use the criteria we agreed on to assess your work. After you do your presentations, I will ask each group to self-assess. I will also be using the criteria we developed to give feedback. Any questions?

Some students know what teachers want without it ever being made explicit. It seems others simply don't get it. When we make the criteria explicit, share the process of learning with each other, and give descriptive feedback according to the agreed criteria, we give more students the opportunity to learn. We begin to make more of the implicit expectations explicit.

When we give students a chance to share their knowledge with each other and with us, they learn and we learn. Celebrating our accomplishments by sharing our work with others is part of the process of learning. The audience can be other people in the class, other classes, parents and guardians, or community members. When the learning is captured in print, on videotape or audiotape, or electronically, it becomes concrete evidence that can be used later, when students conference and report to others.

Self-Assessment and Goal-Setting

> As you think about your work, I want you to review the criteria we set together. Take a few moments and write in your journal what you noticed you were able to do well and two things you need to work on next.

When students and teachers self-assess, they confirm, consolidate, and integrate new knowledge. Debriefing after the learning provides an opportunity for collaborative feedback—from student and teacher perspectives. What do we think we learned? What worked? What didn't? What might we do differently next time?

Self-Assessment Activities

Some self-assessment activities take a few minutes for students to complete, while others are more complex and involve a variety of steps. Self-assessment activities [can be organized] under three headings:

- *Pause and Think:* Students assess their work by taking a few minutes to pause and think or reflect about what they are learning.

- *Look for Proof:* Students go one step beyond pause-and-think activities; they select a work sample as proof of an aspect of their learning and comment about their work.

- *Connect to Criteria:* Students assess their work in relation to criteria that have been set for a task or project and find evidence to show they have met the criteria.

From Gregory, Cameron, and Davies, *Self-Assessment and Goal-Setting*, 9–10.

When students self-assess, they gain insights about their learning. These insights help them monitor their learning and provide practice in giving themselves descriptive feedback. When student self-assessments are shared with teachers, teachers gain a better understanding about where students are in relation to where they need to be.

Revisiting Criteria

Now that you have completed the research project, it is time to revisit the criteria we set. I noticed that some groups did things which weren't on our T-chart. Your presentations and projects may have reminded you of other things that make a research project powerful. Does anyone have any ideas about what needs to be added, changed, or taken away?

As students learn and assess, they define and redefine the criteria, each time making them more specific. Criteria become more specific because students are learning more about high-quality work. It is important that the criteria allow for the many different ways students may select to represent the results of their research. For example, the same criteria should be able to be used effectively for a timeline, a poster, a written project, or a model. Using criteria that allow for a range of representation encourages students to represent what they know in a variety of ways, and gives teachers a way to fairly assess a variety of projects.

Setting Goals

> Please look at the criteria and your self-assessment, and think about what you need to focus on the next time. This will become your goal. Do not take on too many things. One or two goals are about all anyone can handle. Record one or two goals, what your first steps are going to be, and who you are going to partner with for support.

When students work together to set criteria, self-assess, and reset criteria, they come to understand the process of assessment and begin to learn the language of assessment. Students gain a clear picture of what they need to learn and where they are in relation to where they need to be, and they get an opportunity to begin to identify possible next steps in their learning. Setting goals is a powerful way to focus students' learning.

Exit Pass

Two things I learned . . .

- using juicy words

- cutting my notes into strips

One question I have . . .

- Can I show you my plan tomorrow?

Adapted from Gregory, Cameron, and Davies, *Self-Assessment and Goal-Setting*, 18.

Ongoing Self-Assessment and Goal-Resetting

> Class, before you leave today, I'd like you to fill out the card on your desk. Let me know two things you've learned about research projects and one question you have. Thank you.

When we think about what we've done, we may come to understand it in a different way. Self-assessment gives learners the opportunity to think about their thinking and their learning—a process called *metacognition*. Michael Fullan puts it this way: "An event is not an experience until you reflect upon it." When students share their thinking with teachers, teachers can teach better.

Sharing the Work

Linking assessment and learning in this way results in students learning the *how* of learning as much as the learning itself. Involving students in assessment leads to more student ownership and investment in the learning than when the responsibility for assessment (and for learning) rests entirely with the teacher.

- When students are involved in their own assessment, they are required to think about their learning and articulate their understanding, which helps them learn. (Schon 1983, 1990; Walters, Seidel, and Gardner 1994; Wolf 1987, 1989; Young 2000; Zessoules and Gardner 1991)

- Self-assessment asks students to make choices about what to focus on next in their learning. When students make choices about their learning, achievement increases; when choice is absent, learning decreases. (Purkey and Novak 1984; deCharms 1968, 1972; Kovalik 1994; Lepper and Greene 1974, 1978; Maehr 1974; Mahoney 1974; Deci and Ryan 1985; Deci, Vallerand, Pelletier, and Ryan 1991; Mager and McCann 1963)

- When students are involved in their own assessment, mistakes become feedback they can use to adjust what they are doing. When students' mistakes are identified by others and feedback limited to marks or letters, students are less likely to know what to do differently next time. (Butler and Nisan 1986, 1987; Butterworth and Michael 1975; Kohn 1993; Seagoe 1970; Shepard and Smith 1986, 1987)

- Involving students in assessment and increasing the amount of descriptive feedback while decreasing evaluative feedback increases student learning significantly. While all students show significant gains, students who usually achieve the least show the largest gains overall. (Black and Wiliam 1998)

As students become more involved in the assessment process, teachers find themselves working differently. They used to be solely responsible for providing information about the learning. Now there are as many references for students to use as there are models, exemplars, samples, posted criteria, and peers. Many teachers are spending less time marking at the end of the learning and more time helping students during the learning. As teachers find more ways to involve students and increase the amount of descriptive feedback while decreasing the evaluative feedback, they are discovering for themselves what Black and Wiliam (1998) found in their research—students are learning more.

Rethinking

Thanks to research and theory concerning learning, intelligence, the brain, the role of emotions, and what it means to be a self-directed learner, we are rethinking the role of classroom assessment in supporting student learning.

As we see ways to make classroom assessment work, we are asking how we can:

- build a foundation for assessment in our classrooms (Chapter 2)
- help students understand what they are to learn (Chapter 3)

- use samples to show what the learning could look like (Chapter 4)
- decide what counts as evidence (Chapter 5)
- use assessment to guide instruction (Chapter 6)
- involve students in collecting, organizing, and presenting evidence (Chapter 7)
- involve students in communicating about learning (Chapter 8)
- involve students and parents in evaluating and reporting (Chapter 9)
- deepen our own understanding and the understanding of others about classroom assessment (Appendix)

As you work with the ideas in this book, consider yourself invited to develop your own expertise in the area of classroom assessment. On a CBC broadcast in 1994, Canadian journalist and author Rita Shelton Deverell defined an expert as "A person who has a deep understanding of their own personal experience." As you think through the issues, become familiar with the research, make your decisions, and work with students and colleagues, you will find your own ways to make classroom assessment work better for you and for your students. It will be like building your own Inukshuk.

Building Your Inukshuk

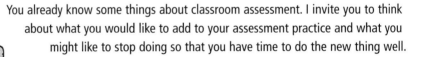

You already know some things about classroom assessment. I invite you to think about what you would like to add to your assessment practice and what you might like to stop doing so that you have time to do the new thing well.

1. Begin by thinking about what you have read so far. Has it confirmed some things for you? Did you think "I already do that"? Did it remind you of anything you had forgotten?

2. Highlight something you would like to learn more about. Record your ideas and perhaps talk with someone else about your thinking.

Chapter ②

Building the Foundation for Classroom Assessment

Evaluation is multi-faceted—it has to be because of the very nature and complexity of the child or program it seeks to evaluate.

Norma Mickelson

Building a classroom environment that supports learning involves finding out who your students are, letting them find out who you are, and establishing classroom agreements about how everyone will work and learn together.

In order to fully participate in their learning and assessment, students need a foundation. Students need to understand:

- mistakes are essential for learning
- the difference between descriptive and evaluative feedback
- that they will have the time to try out their ideas
- that success has many different looks

Mistakes are Essential for Learning

Learning involves taking risks and making mistakes, and then doing things differently as a result. Mistakes provide assessment evidence—they give learners feedback about what is not working and bring them closer to knowing what will work. Unless students understand that mistakes are essential for learning, they may not take necessary risks.

Dewey (1933) referred to learning and reflecting on the learning (self-assessment) as a continuous cycle—a learning loop—we learn, we assess, we learn some more. Now, almost 80 years later, the research about the brain is again pointing to the critical need for self-assessment in all learning. The brain is *self-referencing*. That is, we decide what to do next based on an assessment of what we have just done.

When teachers model making mistakes and fixing them, students learn to value their own mistakes as a source of information for their learning. They begin to view mistakes as feedback that shows them what they need to do differently. When we create a classroom community that is safe for learners, they are more likely to take risks necessary for learning. This type of community develops when learners know how to give help, how to get help, what help to get, and how to use the help to improve their learning.

Understanding Feedback

Learners understand feedback. It is what they get when they try to shoot a basket and make it or don't make it. It is what happens when someone laughs as they share a funny story. It is what the teacher gives when you finish an assignment or turn in your homework. What students don't usually understand is that there are different types of feedback—descriptive feedback and evaluative feedback (Sutton 1997).

Criteria for MAP	Sample Match
- easy to read and find the places	Closest match is sample # _2_ because…
	- it's easy to read
- locations are accurately labelled/placed	- you misplaced the Danube River
	- you missed the Atlantic Ocean
- nothing is missing	
Conference requested ☐	Question(s):
Date(s) received: Oct. 1	
Assessed by ☑ teacher ☐ self ☐ partner ☐ other	Assignment: Map #3 Europe Student: Jamie G., Block E

From Gregory, Cameron, and Davies, *Setting and Using Criteria*, 37.

Descriptive Feedback

Descriptive feedback tells students about their learning—what is working (do more of this) and what is not (do less of this). They can use this information to adjust what they're doing to be more successful and to learn from their mistakes.

Since many teachers find it difficult to give students enough descriptive feedback, they make available other sources of feedback for students, such as posted samples or criteria created with students. Students can also give themselves descriptive feedback when they compare their work to models, posted samples, or detailed criteria. They also receive descriptive feedback when classmates use criteria to describe one specific thing that met the criteria and one question they have.

Descriptive feedback:

- comes during as well as after the learning
- is easily understood and relates directly to the learning
- is specific, so performance can improve
- involves choice on the part of the learner as to the type of feedback and how to receive it
- is part of an ongoing conversation about the learning
- is in comparison to models, exemplars, samples, or descriptions
- is about the performance or the work—not the person

Evaluative Feedback

Evaluative feedback tells the learner how she or he has performed as compared to others (norm-referenced assessment) or what was to be learned (criterion-referenced assessment). Evaluative feedback is often reported using letters, numbers, checks, or other symbols. Because evaluative feedback has commonly been encoded, students usually understand whether or not they need to improve. But unless descriptive feedback is also provided, students do not have enough information to understand what they need to do in order to improve.

The research shows that evaluative feedback gets in the way of many students' learning (Black and Wiliam 1998; Kohn 1999). When students understand what needs to be learned and are involved in gathering evidence of their learning, then it is easier for them to see evaluation as part of the learning process rather than as a defining moment describing success or failure. Teachers seeking to improve student learning are advised by researchers (Black and Wiliam 1998; Kohn 1993) to reduce the amount of evaluative feedback and increase the amount of descriptive feedback.

Taking Time to Learn

In order to learn, students need time to process. This is because meaning (learning) is only generated from within (Jensen 1998). When we have more time to think about our learning, we learn more. Sometimes, pressured to cover the curriculum in the time we have, we don't take time to let students do the processing they need to do in order to learn. When students talk about their learning and self-assess in relation to criteria, models, or exemplars, they are giving themselves descriptive feedback that helps them learn more.

Some people picture learning as students sitting quietly, listening. That is only a small part of what needs to happen for learning to take place. When students are "thinking, problem-solving, constructing, transforming, investigating, creating, analyzing, making choices, organizing, deciding, explaining, talking and communicating, sharing, representing, interpreting, assessing, reflecting, taking responsibility, exploring, asking and answering, recording, predicting, gaining new knowledge and applying that knowledge to new situations" they are learning (Cameron et al. 1997, 6). These all take time because they all involve processing. Jensen (1998) explains that it is only when external stimuli (such as the teacher) are shut down that learning becomes possible.

Teachers are realizing that when they "slow down to the speed of learning" and involve students, then students are more likely to know what they are to learn and what it looks like (Cameron 1999). When students have time to think about their learning—self-assess—and decide what needs to be changed or improved, then they can set goals. Students need time to:

- set and use criteria
- self-assess
- receive and give descriptive feedback
- collect proof or evidence of learning
- set and reset their goals
- seek support for their learning
- communicate their learning to others

"Well-formulated goals lead to action; they offer more than wishes and hopes."

(Preece 1995, 37)

It takes time to involve students in the assessment process. Start slowly. Students will believe we value their words and their contributions when they see, hear, and watch us valuing them.

Recognizing Success

Students have a better chance of being successful if they know what success looks like. For example, we cannot assume that students know what a good presentation or retelling looks like. There is too much room for miscommunication when we use only words.

There are many ways to help students understand and recognize success. We can ask those who have knowledge or ideas to demonstrate what something means or might look like. We can bring in guests to perform (such as another class who has already been practising a particular skill), watch videos of other classes, or look at student work from previous years. These all give reference points, models, and exemplars for the learning.

Students also need access to a range of samples of what success looks like along the way, such as three different writing samples showing development in paragraph writing over time, or four different ways students presented their research findings in previous years. Showing students a range of samples sends the message that their job, no matter where they are in their learning, is to get better by learning more. We acknowledge for students that learning is a continuous process and that everyone learns in different ways and at different rates. If we present learning as something all students do in the same way at the same time, we risk having some students not see any possibility for their success. Others may not have the information they need to get better, and others may be unfairly excluded from showing what they know. We risk their learning and their future success.

We also need to invite students to think about different ways they could give proof that they have learned something. This allows for different learning styles and different ways of representing what has been learned. This increases opportunities for students to use all of their knowledge, skills, and experience.

Together, through conversations and looking at samples, students and teachers can define the many looks of success. When students and teachers talk together in classrooms about what something looks and sounds like, they build a shared vocabulary—a shared language for assessment. Students can use the language of assessment to self-assess and manage their own learning. Without this shared language and vision of success, students may not understand, use, or be assisted in their learning through the classroom assessment process.

Involving Parents

Part of the foundation for classroom assessment is effective communication with parents. Three of the ways teachers build relationships that extend beyond the classroom are invitations to share information, goal-setting conferences, and checking in. The sooner we begin the better.

Invitations to Share

Many teachers telephone parents or invite them to write letters describing their children as learners (Jovanovic 1979; Calkins 1991). Others call ahead and arrange home visits or invite students and parents to visit the classroom before school begins. Whatever approach teachers choose, they receive helpful information about students and their learning outside of school as well as a better appreciation for the context of students' learning. Many parents appreciate the invitation to help you understand what their son or daughter brings to the learning.

Goal-Setting Conferences

Another way to build successful learning communities is to invite parents and guardians to participate in goal-setting conferences. In goal-setting conferences, students and parents first meet at home and talk about strengths and areas needing improvement. They set learning goals together. The student and parents then meet with the teacher and tell the teacher about the student as a learner. The teacher takes notes and asks questions. From this process, teachers get powerful information about students as learners, and students and parents are heard.

Here's how one teacher describes the process and benefits of goal-setting conferences in his elementary class.

> Every year we have a meeting with the parents about what the students are going to be learning. A few years ago we started having the parents bring the children. Last year I decided that we were missing an opportunity to find out more about the kids as learners. I wanted the parent and child to think about what the child was good at and what they needed to work on, as well as what kinds of goals they wanted to achieve during the year. I gave each student a sheet to take home. It was sort of like a survey for the child and the parent. The students had to think about what they were really good at, what they were really proud of, what they wanted to get better at, and how they could help themselves learn. The parents were asked to write about the same

things and to say how they could help their child. I asked them to bring along anything they wanted me to see.

It was amazing. When they came for their conferences, I got to listen to students talk about themselves as learners. The parents were so impressed. I listened to the parents talk about the child as a learner. The students just beamed. I asked questions and took notes. I found out so many things that I don't think I would ever have found out if I hadn't asked. It helped me when I was preparing for different units because I knew some of the kids knew more than I ever would. Also a couple of kids who weren't great at school had amazing talents—talents they were known for outside of school, such as being able to fix all kinds of small engines. Because I knew all about these incredible talents and expertise, I was able to help them gain equal status in our class.

For the conferences, I gave people 20-minute time slots—we met at lunch, after school, and one evening. I also used the open-house-night time. It was worth every minute. Next year our staff is talking about moving one of the conference days to early in the year so we can all do these kinds of conferences.

Checking In

Rather than waiting to figure out what is going on and relying solely on your own professional assessments (which can take many months if you wait to gather enough data to be sure), everyone benefits if you check initial assessments with students and parents.

After you complete your initial assessments at the beginning of the year, consider checking with students and parents if something doesn't make sense, or if students are significantly behind in their learning. (More than two years behind usually means involving our colleagues and putting an intervention plan in place to support the student's learning.)

When you are trying to make sense of the evidence you collect during the year, consider checking with students and parents. Take your assessment findings to the student and say, "This is what I see. Does it make sense to you?" Go to the parents and say, "This is what I see. What do you see? Am I on track here?"

A Community of Learners

Students, parents, and teachers can build a community where learning is supported by assessment only when making mistakes, giving and receiving feedback, and taking time to self-assess and to learn are viewed as essential parts of the learning and assessment process. Only when we work together can the foundation for classroom assessment—and learning—be established.

Building Your Inukshuk

1. Think of a time you learned something successfully. Make some notes about what you learned, when and where you learned it, who helped you, how they helped, and what kind of feedback you got.

   Think about what your experiences tell you about feedback that supports learning. How can you use this information to help your students learn more? How can you begin to give up responsibility for being the main source of feedback in the classroom? How could you create opportunities for students to get descriptive feedback from a variety of sources?

2. Talk with others about your experiences. Build a common list of the kinds of feedback that you found supportive for learning. Talk about the implications for your students' learning and your teaching.

3. You might also find it helpful to read pages 30 to 49 in *Knowing What Counts: Setting and Using Criteria* (Gregory, Cameron, and Davies 1997) and pages 12 to 38 in *Knowing What Counts: Self-Assessment and Goal-Setting* (Gregory, Cameron, and Davies 2000) to explore other ways you might involve students in self-assessment and increase the descriptive feedback students receive.

Chapter ③

Beginning with the End in Mind

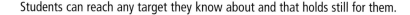

Students can reach any target they know about and that holds still for them.

Richard Stiggins

When golfers swing their golf clubs, they know where to aim—toward the flag in the next hole. Pilots file flight plans before getting permission to leave the ground. Successful gardeners plan for a new season, knowing what they want their garden to look like. It seems obvious that reaching a destination is easier if you know where or what it is. That's the point Tyler (1949) was making over 50 years ago when he said the first question teachers need to answer is, What do you want students to learn? Answering that question has been harder than we thought.

In most educational jurisdictions part of a teacher's job is to assess how well students have learned what they are to learn. This task is part of criterion-referenced assessment. We no longer compare or rank students as we did when we were asked to do norm-referenced assessment in the past. Now we identify clearly what students are to learn and what success looks like, and we make judgments about how well students have learned what they are to learn.

Unfortunately, this information about what the learning looks like isn't always communicated to students. Many students turn up in our classrooms every day and try to do their best without knowing what they need to learn—they have neither a flag, a flight plan, nor a vision of success. If students don't know what they are to learn and what it can look like, they are handicapped and their success is at risk. Some students seem to just get it—they know what you want them to learn before you do. Other students don't. This is especially a problem for those students who typically have the most trouble achieving success in our classrooms.

> "Assessments that work in the best interests of children will enhance their ability to see and understand their learning for themselves, to judge it for themselves, and to act on their judgments."
>
> (Drummond 1994)

We know that advance organizers for a lesson or task help everyone do better and learn more. A simple but interesting study reported by Restak (1988) confirms this. A group of college students were divided into two equal groups. One group was told to go sit in a room and answer the questions they were asked. The other group was told that they would be asked to sit in a chair, look at a screen, and identify the symbols they were shown. Which group did better? The second group. Researchers attributed this group's success to more of their brain being engaged in solving the task—thanks to the advance organizer.

Researchers reporting brain-based research (Langer 1997; Pinker 1997; Jensen 1998; Sylwester 1995; and Restak 1988, 1991) say that when we know what we're going to be doing, we mentally prepare ourselves and activate more of our brain by doing so. Once students know what they are supposed to be learning, they can self-monitor, make adjustments, and learn more. From the teacher's point of view, there are three steps to this process:

- Describe what students need to learn in language students and parents will understand.
- Share the description with students and explain how it relates to success in life outside of school.
- Use the description to guide instruction, assessment, and evaluation.

The focus of this chapter is on how to develop a clear description of the learning.

Describing What Needs to Be Learned

Teachers find that a description of what needs to be learned helps students learn more. While an educational system may define the learning in broad terms through its documents, teachers must translate and summarize the hundreds of statements into language students and parents can understand.

Teachers develop descriptions by analyzing curriculum documents, descriptions of standards and expectations, and professional standards documents such as NCTM Mathematics Standards. They add to this their personal reflections on their own professional experience.

For most people, writing descriptions of learning goals is harder than it looks—words easily obscure meaning. So, start small. Choose one subject area or one unit of study for a focus. Summarize the outcomes or goals in simple, clear language that makes sense given how you will later be required to report. Read and review the curriculum expectations for your subject and grade level, checking back to the documents to see if there is anything you missed.

The following example shows one group's first draft of describing the learning for Grade 7 French. The left column is not a list of the actual learning outcomes from the curriculum document, but instead the teachers' initial summary. Even at this early stage, these teachers found it useful to think ahead and consider possible sources of evidence.

Using the Descriptions

Teachers have many different ways of designing their descriptions to make them easy to use during the year and to align them with school and district reporting requirements (Hurford 1998; Gregory, Cameron, and Davies 1997). Descriptions vary from place to place because the context differs, and each jurisdiction tends to use terms differently. Only you know how to best communicate to colleagues, students, and parents in your school community.

French 7

Learning Outcomes	Possible Evidence
① willingly participates in all activities (esp. oral)	① checklist (observation)
② willingly takes risks	② volunteers consistently (instead of being asked)
③ positive attitude towards a 2nd language, culture	③ by observation
④ shows practice of vocabulary and structures	④ tests, quizzes, daily work
⑤ works cooperatively with partners +/or small groups	⑤ observation – product production – group evaluation
⑥ shows independence in learning ie/uses resources	⑥ looks in Fr/Eng dictionary before asking
⑦ can demonstrate learning visually, orally, and in writing	⑦ projects, assignments, presentations
⑧ makes connections outside of classroom + subject area	⑧ observations and projects

Adapted from material developed at a workshop in Nanaimo, B.C., 1998.

Few teachers begin with a blank slate—we make decisions based on the realities of our work. And we all make different decisions based on the contexts we have for our work. Here are some examples of ways teachers develop and use descriptions of learning.

➤ Mrs. H has to prepare a narrative report card for her early primary class at the end of each term. As part of her assessment and evaluation process, she has reviewed all the documents related to reading and summarized them on an 11-by-17-inch sheet. She shows this sheet to students and explains what it is. She also posts it for parents to see. This summary of what needs to be learned assists her in tracking her students' learning. Later, it is a valuable resource for the three-way conference held at the end of the term and for the narrative report card she prepares for each student.

➤ Mr. R teaches Grade 4. He has to report using a report card that includes a developmental continuum. He makes a copy of the report card and uses the developmental continuum as a summary guide of the elements that he needs to teach and assess. He shares this with students and parents so they all know what he is assessing.

➤ Mr. M uses a three-way reporting process in his Grade 6 class. In this process students do self-reports, the teacher does a report, and the parents review the evidence and are also invited to report. In order that students (and parents) are prepared to be a part of the reporting process, Mr. M has a description of what students will be learning in each mathematics strand. He posts the description at the beginning of each unit. Students also collect evidence related to each part of the description so they will be ready to show their parents the evidence during their conference.

➤ Ms G teaches Grade 9 English. Although she agrees with research that shows that letter grades get in the way of learning (see page 72 of this book), she is still required to give letter grades, and so she does. She tries to "compensate for the compulsory" by being clear with students about what is expected and what success looks like. She drafts a description of what success looks like in Grade 9 English. This description is a series of statements describing what students are to know and be able to do.

Description of Learning
Grade 9 English

- Reads a great deal of challenging material, often of complex style and form, at an independent level.

- Uses a wide variety of reading strategies to deal with different genres. Understands material at both a literal and an inferential level.

- Responds with a deep and insightful understanding, making powerful connections to his or her own life, the lives of others, and to other texts.

- Writes effectively on a range of topics using styles and forms appropriate to a variety of purposes and audiences.

- Consistently follows rules and conventions for spelling, punctuation, and sentence structure.

- Works productively in groups and as part of the class.

Adapted from Gregory, Cameron, and Davies, *Setting and Using Criteria*, 52.

The Development Cycle

Teachers develop descriptions that take into account what needs to be learned and how the learning needs to be reported. Developing and using descriptions is part of the assessment-learning cycle. When we explain to students what they need to learn and answer their questions, they gain a better understanding of what counts. When the descriptions of what needs to be learned are accompanied by samples that show what success looks like, students begin to be informed enough to make choices to help their learning. Then, when students know what the evidence can look like, they become more able to show us what they know in ways we can assess. As we use descriptions in classrooms, we find ways to express them more clearly—an ongoing process with each new group of students and parents.

Here is a summary of how to draft your description, then two ways to work with others to develop your ideas. Revisit and revise your description—always consider it a work in progress.

Draft Your Description

1. To begin, choose one subject area or one unit of study for a focus.
2. Summarize the outcomes or goals in simple, clear language that makes sense given how you will later be required to report.
3. Read and review the curriculum expectations for your subject and grade level and check to see if your description is accurate.

Development Idea 1

1. Check your draft description with colleagues, someone who does not work in education, and/or your students. Ask for feedback.
2. Use your description for one reporting period. Watch what happens.

Development Idea 2

1. Meet with others and compare your descriptions. Talk about differences. Ask others to help you say what needs to be said in the simplest possible way.
2. Pilot your description with a group of students. Ask them if it helps and how it could be better.
3. Write about your experience.
4. Return to your colleagues and talk about your experiences and your learning.

Chapter ④

Showing What the Learning Looks Like

It is important that we use language related to progress, such as beginning, developing, needs assistance to, rather than language related to failure, such as weak, inadequate, or undeveloped.

Caren Cameron and Kathleen Gregory

"What do you want?" says a student. "How good is good enough?" asks a colleague. "What does excellence look like?" you wonder. These are questions that relate to standards. A standard serves as the basis by which work is judged. Different educators and education systems define standards in different ways. *The Canadian Oxford Dictionary* (1998) defines *standard* as "an object or quality or measure serving as basis or example or principle to which others . . . should conform or by which . . . others [are] judged; the degree of excellence required for a particular purpose."

Standards are set by educational systems in many different ways and by involving a variety of people such as educators, parents, and members of the community. They are an expression of what *all* students should know and be able to do. Standards are usually a description of what success looks like in words or numbers. In Chapter 3 we discussed developing a description of what needs to be learned. When we develop standards, we begin to define what success looks like. Teachers may be involved in developing standards or in finding effective ways to use and interpret standards developed by others.

Problems with Standards

There are two parts to effective standards: the description of what success looks like in words and numbers and the samples that illustrate this. Developing and using standards are difficult to do and there are often problems.

One problem is that provincial or state standards often define what students need to learn and be able to do without showing what it looks like. For example, "communicates effectively in writing" looks different for a seven-year-old than for a sixteen-year-old. We may know the standard is "communicates effectively in writing" but have no idea what it looks like for students in a particular age range. If we don't know what the standard looks like, then we won't know when our students have reached it.

Another problem is that standards seem to assume that all students start in the same place, at the same time, and proceed to learn in the same way. Learning is not sequential. Students learn in different ways and at different rates. A three-year range in development is normal (Jensen 1998). Students in a class will never be all the same. Standards that ignore this reality can get in the way of many students' learning and make classroom evaluation difficult. Diversity is a source of strength in our communities, and it is also a source of strength in our classrooms.

Also, an effort to define standards so that they are easily understood sometimes results in too closely linking what students are to know with the way in which they show their learning. If we ask students to show what they understand about World War II, we may get a range of evidence from a play to a timeline to a photo history. If we ask them to take a test or write an essay, then we have unnecessarily limited the opportunity for all students to show what they know. If our purpose was to assess how well they could write an essay, then an essay is the evidence that would make sense. But demonstrating understanding requires a range of evidence.

Making Standards Work

So how can standards be used to help *all* students learn? By ensuring that standards are accompanied by a range of samples that show what development might look like over time. Standards can be informed by good-quality large-scale assessments that may provide useful information about the range of what students know and are able to do at different ages. When teachers and students know where they are going, they are more likely to achieve success. Standards used in this way can become a guide for our teaching and for student learning.

Knowing what the range of evidence of learning looks like at different developmental points makes the learning destination more clear. For example, if we want our students to know what "communicates effectively in writing" looks like, we need to show them writing samples that show a range of development, including samples that are within their grasp and just beyond.

Student samples take many forms, including maps, reading responses, writing, projects, mathematical thinking, problem-solving, videos of oral presentations or research projects—anything that illustrates what students are expected to know and do in the classroom. Samples of student work illustrate the description of learning and answer the question, "What will it look like when I've learned it?"

Collections that illustrate standards can be developed by working with colleagues to gather and analyze samples. Samples can then be used to:

• develop criteria with students
• show the range of possible ways to represent their learning (give evidence)
• assess and give descriptive feedback about student work
• help parents understand more about student learning

Here are some ways teachers have used samples to support classroom assessment.

 Ms. J decided that one way to illustrate standards for reading in Grade 2 was to put together a collection of book titles and authors that show the range of what students at this level read. She based her collection on her own experience and suggestions from colleagues. She posted the list on the school Web site so parents could refer to it from time to time as their child progressed.

Mr. V gathered work from his Grade 4 students and from colleagues to make files of six to ten samples that show the range of writing children of this age can produce in each of the following three general categories:

• personal experience
• narratives
• communicating information

Mr. T worked with his students to put together a large collection of products that shows a range of mathematical thinking and problem-solving at the Grade 7 level. These include:

• journal entries that show problem-solving
• notebooks (including some from previous years)
• "before" and "after" portfolio entries
• sample questions that students designed for partners to solve

➡ Over the past three years, Ms. B has built a collection of samples that shows the range of reading and writing that students in Grade 11 can do. These include:

- reader response journal entries
- lists of books read by students
- sample paragraphs
- projects (posters, literary maps, character analyses, oral presentations on videotape)

➡ Ms. D teaches a fifth-year university history course. She collects a range of samples of assignments from some students each term as well as some of the final exam questions and answers. Each assignment has a performance grid (developed with students) attached. Although there are no column labels, letter grades or scaled numbers as headings, it is clear from the description that the level of quality changes from column to column. The discussion with students gives them a sense of the different looks quality work can have at this level. She is careful to ensure that the descriptions at each level provide descriptive (not evaluative) feedback. For example, the description might say "needs to be edited for spelling" (descriptive feedback) rather than "lots of spelling errors" (evaluative feedback). Students are able to resubmit assignments up until a few days before final grades are assigned.

➡ Mr. R is a learning resource teacher in an elementary school setting. He has a collection of student writing samples, from drawings with letter-like forms to student-written chapter books, showing writing development. He has put them into an accordion-style construction-paper booklet that can be kept on a bookshelf but unfolds to create a long display, like a frieze.

Collecting and Analyzing Samples

Teachers can collect samples themselves over time, but it is easier and more powerful if done with colleagues. The process of analyzing and selecting samples gives teachers the chance to see a broad range of student work, understand what students are to know, develop a commonly held sense of what the learning might look like for students over time, and begin to develop a common language to use.

Here is one process you could follow:

1. Find some interested and willing colleagues.
2. Choose a focus for your investigation (e.g., journal writing).
3. Collect a range of samples. (Ensure that they are anonymous.)
4. Analyze what is working and what the next teaching steps could be for each sample. Compare your student samples to exemplars provided by provincial or state assessments, if available.
5. Build a personal collection.
6. Choose another focus and repeat the cycle.

Here are some descriptions of how others have worked to gather samples. In some cases the samples from provincial and state assessments were used to clarify understanding of standards; in some cases they were used to actually establish standards for educational jurisdictions. In all cases, students' names were removed from the samples.

A Teacher Leads

Mr. M, new to middle school and unsure of what kind of Readers' Theatre students of this age were capable of, put out a request asking teachers to share any samples of scripts or videos of performances they might have collected over the years. He offered to copy and collate the collection, as well as to later add his students' work to the collection. Three teachers responded, permissions were obtained, and a collection of samples and videotaped presentations was made and distributed.

Whole-School Participation

One school wanted to learn more about what good writing looked like for students of different ages. They all agreed to collect first-draft journal-writing samples that showed the range of writing in their class and to bring at least six samples to the next meeting.

Copies were made of the samples so everyone could look at them. Sitting in grade-level groups, the teachers looked at all the samples, talked about what was typical for this age range, what was outstanding, and what would be of concern. They selected some from the entire group of samples that showed the range of what students were able to do at their grade level.

Record Sheet for Student Samples

Sample number:_____ Age of student in years and months (if known):_____

Context or Task
What kind of writing was the student asked to do?

_____

Support
How much support was given to the student (if known)?

_____

Analysis
What does this student know how to do as a writer? Consider the points on the following chart.

Description	Analysis
Meaning What is the writer attempting to convey?	
Style, Personal Expression What kinds of words and sentences does the writer use?	
Form What kind of organization does the writer use? What kinds of writing conventions?	
Surface Features What is the writer able to do in terms of sentence structure and spelling?	
Next Steps On the basis of what you see here, what are the next instructional steps for this student?	

After members of grade-level groups had analyzed and selected samples, they listed what the students knew how to do as writers at each level. A recorder took notes. They also brainstormed one or two possible "next steps" in terms of instruction, based on the needs evident in each sample.

Near the end of the three-hour period, the teachers reviewed the work samples of students from the youngest to the oldest in the school, in order to have a sense of development over time. The writing samples were collected and placed in a binder for teachers and parents. Later, the education department published a collection of writing samples, and the group reviewed them and added the additional samples to their collection.

The next topic staff chose to learn more about was reading development. They did this by collecting reader responses from a wide range of students. They also involved staff from a neighbouring school, which increased the breadth of expertise of the reviewers and the range of student samples. Both schools got a copy of the samples and the analysis.

A Provincial or State-Level Committee

After analyzing large numbers of writing samples, a provincial committee developed a description of writing development from K to 12. In order to help teachers understand the description of writing development, the committee collected samples from across the province to illustrate what students know and are able to do at different ages—development over time from kindergarten to graduation. The samples were selected to show the *range* of development that could be expected at different ages.

Using the Samples

Samples of student work are most often used in three ways:

- to develop criteria with students
- to help assess student work
- to help others understand learning

Developing Criteria with Students

Collections of student samples illustrate for teachers what students can do and help students develop a sense of what is important. When students analyze samples, they begin to understand what student work looks like at different points on its way to the standard. They also begin to internalize the criteria that will be used to assess their work. When students understand what is important, they have an opportunity to assess their own efforts in regard to the criteria and give themselves feedback about their own learning as they progress.

Setting and Using Criteria (Gregory, Cameron, and Davies 1997) outlines a process for developing criteria with students:

1. Make a brainstormed list.
2. Sort and categorize the list.
3. Make and post a T-chart.
4. Use and revisit and revise.

When using samples to develop criteria, students first examine the samples and list the important features. The teacher records their ideas on a brainstormed list, pointing out any features they may have missed. Once the list is complete, the ideas are sorted and transcribed onto a T-chart that can be posted in the class. The list of criteria is then used to give descriptive feedback and assess student work.

Assessing Student Work

If the criteria are clear, then there are many ways to respond to student work and give descriptive feedback "without putting a mark on the paper," such as highlighting which criteria have been met or identifying two next steps (Gregory, Cameron, and Davies 1997). When samples are available, students can compare their work to see what is working or what needs attention.

Readers' Theatre

Criteria	Details
Performers' positions help communicate the message.	- some readers were elevated - audience can see everyone they are supposed to - scripts don't make noise
Performers' voices communicate meaning.	- words are clear (enunciation) - readers voices change to match script and characters - readers can read the script - there aren't any big silences
Performers' actions help audience listen and understand.	- rehearsed - props help audience understand - performers enter and exit smoothly - everyone bows together - people turn when they are supposed to

Adapted from Dixon, Davies and Politano,
Learning with Readers Theatre, 71.

Grant Wiggins (1998) tells about watching a student at work in technology class. The student's project was nearly complete. He put on the final touches and then took it to the table where finished projects were placed. As he set his project down, he noticed something about the display model. He picked up the model and looked it over carefully. He set it down, picked up his own project, and returned to his place to continue work. This is an example of timely, specific, descriptive feedback—yet no teacher was directly involved.

There is no one right way to use samples—teachers use any way that helps students understand what the learning looks like. Here are some examples.

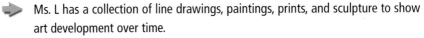 Ms. S asks students to practise their reading in partners. While one partner is reading, the other is observing those things that show he or she is a good reader. The observer has a record sheet the students created that lists characteristics of good reading.

Ms. L has a collection of line drawings, paintings, prints, and sculpture to show art development over time.

Mr. R has a collection of research projects from previous years to show his students what is possible and what success might look like.

Ms. Z posts two or three numbered samples of maps with the criteria that the class developed with her assistance.

Mr. C posts two samples of reader responses to show students the way to quality. While working, students are asked to compare their work to the samples. Later, students may be asked to self-assess in relation to the criteria posted with the samples or to decide which sample their work most resembles and why. This self-assessment is attached to their work and submitted to the teacher.

Helping Others Understand Learning

Showing samples can help teachers answer students' questions—"What do you want?" "How good is good enough?" "What does excellence look like?"—by showing the samples that illustrate the standard. Showing samples and comparing student work can also help answer the parent who asks, "How is my child doing?"

When using samples and exemplars, it is important to continue to acknowledge that students learn in different ways and at different rates. Starting with students and their work and talking with colleagues are ways teachers are making sense of standards. Our job is to be thoughtful and as curious as possible about how our students learn and how to use assessment to support learning.

1. Choose one area of focus and collect a range of student samples. Remove all identifying features. (You may need to trade samples with a colleague at another school. It is essential that students not be able to identify another student's work).

   - Look through the samples and think about what they tell you about development over time.
   - Develop a list of what you see in each sample that is important for students to notice.
   - Ask students to look at the samples and make a list of what they think is important.
   - Collect all ideas and, using the four-step process (see page 31), develop criteria students can use in their work and you can use in your assessment.

2. Taking a teacher-as-researcher point of view, write about your experience. What did you notice? What was helpful? What was not? The most important question to ask yourself is: Did the samples of student work help students learn?

3. Consider inviting students to reflect on the process. Ask your students the same questions. What might you do differently next time?

Chapter ⑤

Evidence of Learning

Only if we expand and reformulate our view of what counts as human intellect will we be able to devise more appropriate ways of assessing it and more effective ways of educating it.

Howard Gardner

Once you have described what students need to learn and have developed a sense of what success might look like for your students, it is time to consider what kinds of evidence you will need to collect in order to plan ongoing instruction and to evaluate at the end of the learning period.

Different teachers collect different kinds of evidence, even though the description of what their students need to learn may be the same. This is because the learning experiences teachers design vary. Also, because students learn in different ways and at different times, collections of evidence may vary slightly in terms of how students choose to represent their learning. When making lists of the evidence to collect, teachers need to make sure they plan to gather evidence from a variety of sources, and that they gather evidence over time.

Sources of Evidence

Reliability: think repeatability — reliability refers to students producing the same kind of result at different times.

Validity: think valid—the extent to which the assessment measures what it was supposed to measure.

There are three general sources of assessment evidence gathered in classrooms: **observations** of learning, **products** students create, and **conversations**—discussing learning with students. When evidence is collected from three different sources over time, trends and patterns become apparent. Collecting information this way is one way the reliability and validity of our classroom assessment is increased. This process is called *triangulation* (Lincoln and Guba 1984).

Triangulation

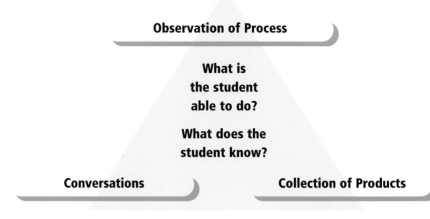

Observation of Process

**What is
the student
able to do?**

**What does the
student know?**

Conversations

Collection of Products

Observing the Learning

The list of evidence you plan to collect needs to include some observations you will make while students are learning. The record of observations becomes evidence.

You might observe . . . formal and informal presentations, drama presentations, scientific method being applied, music-related activities, reading aloud, group or partner activities, talking about one's own work, planning and designing a Web page, persuading, giving opinions, following instructions, listening to others, arguing, predicting, measuring objects, charades, dances, communicating ideas to others in a small group setting, conflict resolution, discussions, giving and receiving descriptive feedback, working with partners or in teams, identifying sounds, rhythm games, cartooning, playing instruments, jigsaws, demonstrations, any skills development, movement exercises, keyboarding, gestures, pantomimes, re-enactments, gymnastic routines, sign language, graphic design, simulations, debating, answering questions, presenting own work, giving instructions, singing, telling stories, verbalizing abstract reasoning, sculpture, choral readings, conversations, dialogues, dramatic readings, oral descriptions, oral reports, plays, puppet shows, Readers' Theatre, storytelling, demonstrating symbolic thinking, teaching a lesson, creating a slide show, role plays, verbal explanations, and verbal instructions. This list could include anything a teacher might see students doing or ask students to do.

Observations are essential if your classroom assessment and evaluation are to be reliable and valid. In addition to being necessary for triangulating your evidence, some learning can only be observed. For example, some students are better able to show what they know by doing it. These "in action" kinds of learners and younger children who are able to record little in writing need some of their learning assessed through observation. Also, products "under construction" can provide teachers with opportunities to observe students' learning. Without enough observational evidence, our findings risk being invalid.

Spelling Focus

- journal writing
- observing prefixes
- and suffixes

✓ observed
—— not observed
0 needs help

Date
Oct. 14, 1999
Nov. 10, 1999

Anna	Bob	Concordia	Carl	Chin	Don	Elaine	Elvin
✓dis, un	✓un, ing	es, dis	dis, re	—	✓ es	—	—
✓	✓	✓	✓	✓dis, re, es, ed	✓	✓ing, ed, es	✓ing, dis, es

Kara	Kevin	Luis	Nona	Matt J.	Matt M.	Parma	Robert
—	✓ing, un	—	—	✓ed	0 ed es consonant doubling	0 ed es c.d.?	✓ex, un
✓un, dis	✓	✓	✓	✓es, re	✓ed, ing es? needs work	✓ed, es, dis, on	✓dis, ed

Ryland	Stefan	Sidura	Thang	Val	Zoe		
✓dis	✓ing, re	✓ed, dis, ing	✓un, ing	—	✓ing, es, ed, un		
✓ed, ing	✓dis, es, ed	✓es, ed	✓es, ed	✓re, es dis, ed	✓re, dis		

From Smith and Davies, *Wordsmithing*, 85.

Teachers have different ways of recording their observations. The key is that observations need to be focused to ensure that the information you are recording is related to the description of what students are to learn. It is usually not enough to observe that a student completed his math work. Rather, you would observe what skill was practiced, what level of skill the student was observed as demonstrating, and perhaps some possible next steps for instruction. For example, if students are practising two-digit addition, you might choose to observe and record the level of difficulty of the questions students choose to practise: addition without regrouping, addition with regrouping. These observations may be used to form your teaching groups the next day, or to determine the subject of your math mini-lesson and the next day's practice activities. The same observations will later form part of the evidence that you will examine when you evaluate the students' progress in mathematics.

The focus of your observations depends on the purpose of the activity. If you can answer the questions below, then you are on your way to designing focused observations that will be useful in planning subsequent learning activities and will form a part of your evaluation later in the term.

- What is the purpose of the learning activity? What are students to learn?
- What particular focus will I choose for this observation?
- How will I record and organize my observations so they are useful?

Collecting Products

Teachers collect various kinds of evidence to show what students can do. These include projects, assignments, notebooks, and tests. As teachers become more knowledgeable about the implications of different theories of intelligence (Gardner 1984; Sternberg 1996), they are expanding the ways students show or represent what they know. When students are asked to represent what they know only in writing, for example, some students will not be able to show what they know because they are not very able as writers. Ask them to demonstrate the process in action or to give an oral presentation, though, and their knowledge and skill may rapidly become apparent.

Different ways to show what we know . . .

- draw a diagram
- make a timeline
- make a poster
- write a story
- do an oral presentation
- write a poem
- build a model
- design a Web page
- create a puzzle
- make a video
- make a tape
- design a T-shirt
- do a report
- write a song
- create a collage
- build a diorama
- write a play
- do a journal entry

More and more teachers are introducing an element of choice in what form products may take. Some teachers create a list of ideas with their students. Over time the list is added to as students learn more about different ways of representing.

Conversations About Learning

Conversations about learning involve listening to what students have to say about their learning. The "conversation" may be face-to-face or in writing.

Conversations can take place during class meetings, at individual or group conferences, or when we read students' self-assessments about their work. We also have opportunities to listen when students assess their work in relation to criteria, analyze their work samples for their portfolios, or prepare to report to parents about their learning.

When we listen to students in these ways, we are inviting them to think about their learning. As they think and explain, we can gather evidence about what they know and understand. We can find out what they did or what they created—their best efforts, what was difficult or easy, what they might do differently next time, and what risks they take as learners. Students learn more when we take the time to involve them in self-assessment (Black and Wiliam 1998; Young 2000).

> Please notice . . . *I read at least 10 pages every day. I read so much on Thursday so I could find out what happened.*
>
> Teacher response: *You are obviously enjoying this, Chris. Can you think of anyone else in our class who would like to read this book when you are done?*

From Gregory, Cameron, and Davies, *Self-Assessment and Goal-Setting*, 26.

Creating a Plan

It takes some planning to make sure you have enough evidence, the right kind of evidence, and evidence that is reliable and valid.

How much evidence is enough?

There is no one right answer to this question. The amount of ongoing evidence needed to effectively plan day-to-day instruction varies from teacher to teacher, depending on the subject, the teacher, the students, and the community in which they learn. Each teacher needs to determine the amount of evidence that works in his or her situation, given what students are learning.

One guideline to keep in mind is that you must have enough evidence to be able to identify trends or patterns in student learning. To do this, you need student work (evidence) that accounts for the full range of what needs to be learned. The evidence needs to show learning over time.

How do I know I have the right kinds of evidence?

The kinds of assessment evidence collected from students need to be appropriate to the type of learning. For example, a paper-and-pencil test is a great way to assess knowledge of basic facts. It wouldn't be an appropriate way to assess oral presentation skills. Sorting out what kind of evidence you need to show different kinds of learning is a necessary step in planning what evidence to collect. If your evidence is triangulated, then you are likely using a range of techniques to gather evidence over time. This is key to having the right kind and balance of evidence. Only you can determine whether or not the evidence satisfactorily addresses the range of what needs to be learned.

How can I be sure my evidence will help my evaluations be reliable and valid?

If you have collected enough evidence and the right kind of evidence, then you can feel confident your evaluations will be reliable and valid. In general, confidence increases when there is a wide range of evidence, and when evidence is collected over time. Remember that everything students do, say, and create is potential evidence. Consider assessing more and evaluating less. We interrupt learning if we evaluate too often, whereas assessment information can guide instruction and support learning.

> ### Taking care . . .
>
> Be aware of the important difference between large-scale and classroom assessment. The purpose of large-scale assessments is two-fold: to help the system be accountable (Are we making the best use of our resources?) and to identify trends (Are students learning? What and how well?). To do this, large-scale assessments collect a small amount of information from a large number of students. Classroom assessment, on the other hand, collects a large amount information from a small number of students. Large-scale assessments are designed to give the system feedback so the system can learn; classroom assessment is designed to give individuals feedback so the individual can learn.
>
> Large-scale assessments are designed to assess what students know and can do in relation to what is to be learned, but they do not collect enough information to give a valid picture of what individual students know and can do in a given subject area.

Triangulation of Evidence
Grade 9 English

Observations

- reading skills
- skills of written expression (including writing-process components)
- listening and speaking skills

Conversations

- student conferences
- self-assessments

Products

- reader response journal
- list of books read
- test scores (vocabulary)
- writing portfolio
- project assessments
- writing sources books
- notebooks

Adapted from Gregory, Cameron, and Davies, *Setting and Using Criteria*, 53.

When you get ready to evaluate and report on how well students are doing in relation to what needs to be learned, you will first need to review the description of learning, check that you have the right kinds of evidence, and use evidence (observations, products, and conversations) to answer the questions: "Did this student learn what she or he needed to learn? How well?"

Develop a Plan for Collecting Evidence

1. Return to your earlier description of what students need to learn in a particular area (see "Building Your Inukshuk," page 24, Chapter 3).

2. Think about the evidence you and your students will be able to collect. Consider observations, products, and conversations. Make a list of the evidence related to the description.

3. Review the list, asking yourself:

- Will my evidence show whether students have learned what they needed to learn?
- Is there any evidence I'm collecting that shows learning for which I am not accountable?
- Am I collecting evidence from three different sources?
- Am I collecting enough evidence to see patterns over time?
- Am I collecting too much evidence? Is there anything I can stop collecting?
- How can my students be involved in collecting and organizing the evidence?

Review with a Colleague

Show your draft evidence list to a trusted colleague. Ask if she or he thinks there is anything you have missed or anything you could delete. Consider the suggestions and make your own decision. Use it with one class, in one subject area. Consider beginning with one reporting period.

When we divide up the responsibility for developing the first draft, everyone benefits—we improve our work and have more confidence in it. Talk about your list of evidence with others in your learning circle and get copies of their work. After your discussions, use the drafts to create your own plan. After you have piloted the process and made adjustments to make it better meet your needs, proceed to do the same for other subject areas or courses for which you are responsible.

Chapter ⑥

Using Assessment To Guide Instruction

Holding a mind to a subject is like holding a ship to its course; it implies constant change of position with unity of direction.

John Dewey

Until this point we've focused on getting ready for classroom assessment: describing the learning and planning to gather evidence. Now it is time to look at the assessment process day by day in classrooms. As you read, notice how involving students in assessment causes assessment to become instruction.

Classroom Clean-Up Time

Ms. M asked her Kindergarten students what they knew about keeping things clean and tidy. The students told stories about helping to clean up at home and in the park.

The teacher explained that there was also a need to clean up in school. She said, "What do you think is important about cleaning up in our classroom?" The students said, "Pick up the toys, put the books on the shelf, put the clothes back in the dress-up box, make sure puppets are in the bin, no papers on the floor, coats are hung up, Plasticine is all away, puzzle pieces are in the right box, Lego in the Lego box, sand toys in the sand box."

The teacher recorded all the contributions on sentence strips. Then she said, "When we clean up today, I want you to notice what else you do." At the end of clean up later that day, she asked them what else was part of clean up. One child said, "Everyone is supposed to help." Another said, "We can't make lots of noise." "And we have to hurry," said another. "Yeah," said another, "we'll miss the bus." The teacher recorded all their additional comments.

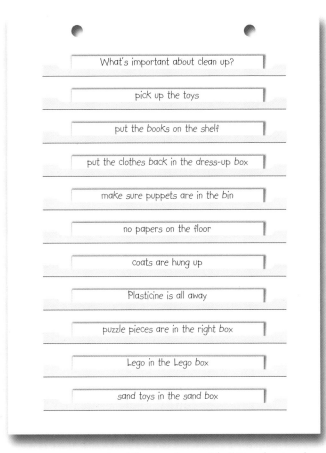

What's important about clean up?

pick up the toys

put the books on the shelf

put the clothes back in the dress-up box

make sure puppets are in the bin

no papers on the floor

coats are hung up

Plasticine is all away

puzzle pieces are in the right box

Lego in the Lego box

sand toys in the sand box

Before clean-up time the next day, the teacher read students their list. Halfway through clean up she called them to the group meeting area and said, "Let's think about how we are doing with clean up. As I read the list again, make the thumbs up sign if you think you are helping in that way." The students listened and put their thumbs up for different items while she read. At the end of the list, the teacher reminded the class about the paint centre and asked them to think about one thing they were going to do to help clean up that area. She also asked them to whisper it to a neighbor, and then they returned to cleaning up.

After clean-up time several days later, the class read the list again. The teacher said, "Our brains have a difficult time remembering all these things. I think we could group them in this way." She moved the strips into groups under the following labels:

- **W**orking Together
- **E**verything in Its Place
- **T**hinking and Acting Safely

The acronym to remind the class was WET. At the end of clean-up time each day the teacher would ask the class to self-assess by asking, "Are we all WET? Did we work together? Is everything in its place? Did we think and act safely?"

Reading Aloud to Others

Mr. F wanted his primary students to focus on oral reading strategies. He began by asking, "What is important when we read aloud?" As the class talked together, they created the following list:

- You can hear their voice easily.
- They show the pictures.
- Your voice goes up and down.
- If the book has a question, your voice has a question in it.
- Read with expression.
- You hold the book so they can see your face.
- You practise first.
- If you get stuck, you can stop and ask for help.
- Read to someone you want to read to.

As students in the class read their practised passages out loud during Reading Club time, the teacher encouraged them to listen and to compliment each reader. The compliments they gave reflected the reader's performance and the listener's understanding of what a good oral reading performance sounds like. Students made comments such as, "You used really good expression," "I liked the way your voice went low when you read the giant's part," or "I liked the way you took a breath at the end of the sentence." If the compliment lacked specificity, such as "It was good" or "You did a good job," the teacher would follow up by asking, "What made it good?" It quickly became a class expectation that compliments would be specific, so the person receiving them would know what exactly he or she had done well.

After they had practised giving compliments, the teacher asked if there was anything else they had noticed about what good readers do when they read out loud. One child said that his dad said to take a break and breathe in when you get to a period. The children discussed this and agreed that was another thing they did sometimes. After this discussion, the teacher used

---

Reading Aloud

Reader's Name: _____

Supporter's Name: _____

As you listen to your partner read, notice the things he or she does that show she or he reads well to others.

❏ You can hear the reader's voice easily.

❏ The reader shows the pictures.

❏ The reader's voice goes up and down (has expression).

❏ If the book has a question, the reader's voice has a question in it.

❏ The reader holds the book so you can see his or her face.

❏ The reader practises first so she or he knows most of the words.

❏ If the reader gets stuck, he or she stops and asks for help.

❏ _____

❏ _____

Adapted from Politano and Davies, *Multi-Age and More*, 88.

the students' ideas to make up a recording sheet. Students used the sheet when they read in partners.

The teacher gave students copies of the recording sheet and explained how to use it with a partner. One person would read while the other person would listen and check off everything she or he saw or heard the reader doing. Then they would change places.

The teacher read a story, and the class practised using the recording sheet by listening to the things he did that showed he was a good reader. Then they worked with partners and practised reading out loud. When they were ready, they used the sheet to record observations about each other's reading. As they learned more about reading aloud, they added more ideas to the list and began to set goals—one thing they were trying to do better. Before they started reading, the reader would ask the observer to watch for evidence of the goal. This became a routine way students gave each other descriptive feedback. The record sheets went into their assessment boxes as evidence.

Research Project

Mrs. C's students were to research a question and then find a way to effectively communicate what they had learned. As they began their research projects, Mrs. C gave a series of mini-lessons to teach them about the research process. She conferenced with different groups of students who were experiencing similar difficulties. The students thought about how they were going to show what they had learned through their research. When they had made their choices in this area, she decided that they were ready to set criteria for an effective research project. She began by having them brainstorm a list titled "What Is Important in a Research Project?" This is part of the list they created:

- pictures
- on topic
- keeps people paying attention
- correct spelling
- interesting sentences
- has beginning, middle, and end
- keep in a safe place
- good describing words
- punctuation (. , ! ? " " ....)
- interesting ideas
- tells what is important

Research Project

Criteria	Details
Organized So Audience Can Follow	- has beginning, middle, and end - keep in a safe place - tells what is important - has a bibliography
Has Interesting Information	- not boring (exciting) - lots of information - brainstorm/web - different sources, like the Internet - sign language, skits, props - uses at least three sources
Keeps Audience Interested and Attending	- pictures, sign language - on topic - keeps people paying attention - could be power point presentation
Edited so Audience Can Understand Easily	- good describing words - punctuation (.,!? " "....) - indented paragraphs - correct spelling - interesting sentences - the form selected helps to communicate the information clearly

The teacher added three other details to the list:

- the form selected helps to communicate the information clearly
- uses at least three sources
- has a bibliography

Once all the ideas were listed, the class sorted them and made a T-chart. The criteria were: organized so audience can follow, has interesting information, keeps audience interested and attending, and edited so audience can understand easily.

The T-chart was photocopied for each student. Their first task was to highlight each word or phrase that was true for their project at this point. If they felt they had completely met any of the criteria on the left they were to write, "met." For the criteria they had not yet met, they were asked to circle one or two details that they were going to work on next and then make a plan for their next steps. They shared their work plans with partners and then set to work. The process of setting criteria and making the end product more clear helped them see where they were in relation to where they needed to be. Most students worked towards meeting all the criteria. Two students with special needs, in consultation with the learning resource teacher and after looking at their Individual Education Plan (IEP), chose one of the four criteria to focus on during this project.

Science Labs

Ms. H used a selection of samples to help prepare her students for writing science lab reports. She selected samples from previous years that were good-quality models of what she was going to be looking for in their lab reports. She made two copies of each science lab, so she had eight samples. She gave one sample to each group of three or four students. They analyzed one sample and then traded and analyzed a second and a third. As they looked at the samples, each group made a list of what makes a really good science lab. After they had enough time to look at two or three samples, the class compiled a whole-class list of criteria. The teacher added two things students hadn't noticed. All the brainstormed ideas were grouped and used to create a T-chart that was posted in the class. The criteria were listed on the left side, and the details that the class had brainstormed were listed on the right side. The three criteria the class developed were: scientific method is complete and easy to follow, data is accurately presented and interpreted, and conclusion(s) is valid.

Criteria for Science Lab Report	Met	Not Yet Met	Please notice ...
- scientific method is complete and easy to follow	✓		I rewrote this twice
- data is accurately presented and interpreted	✓		notice the details in my diagram and I also included a chart this time
- conclusion(s) is valid	✓		

Conference requested ❏   Question(s):

Date(s) received: Oct. 16

Assessed by ❏ teacher   Assignment: Science Lab #4
          ☑ self
          ❏ partner   Student: Aaron D. Block C
          ❏ other

The students wrote up their first lab using the samples as models. Before handing their labs in, the teacher asked them to self-assess, noting which criteria had been met, which were not yet met, and what they wanted the teacher to notice when she assessed their labs. Before doing the next science lab, they reviewed the previous lab with the criteria in mind and selected one thing to improve.

Adapted from Gregory, Cameron, and Davies, *Self-Assessment and Goal-Setting*, 31.

Mathematics

In order to plan for instruction as well as to gather information as part of her initial assessment, Ms. B starts a new year finding out about her students' prior experiences and knowledge. She describes her beginning assessment as follows:

> I find out about their attitude first. I ask them to write about how they feel about math. What are they good at? What do they need to work on? I ask them to tell me about one great memory and one awful memory. I get them writing or talking about what kinds of things I could do to help them. Sometimes I ask them to write a math autobiography. Sometimes, if the group is good with each other, we'll talk about it together. We talk about what they like and don't like about math. I ask them what I could do to make math better and what other people could do. This is sometimes in writing, but other times I meet individually with them, when the class is focusing on something else.

> Sometimes I put a variety of questions on the board and ask them to select the kind of question they do best—so well they could teach others. I ask them to show me how they do those questions. I ask about which questions are the hardest. Why? That tells me some things about the group. Then I ask them to fold a sheet of paper into three. I explain that I want them to show me the easiest question, the question that is really hard for them, and the question that is just about right (it is sort of hard but not really)—just like "Goldilocks and the Three Bears." This gives me an individual look. Then I give them some questions to try with a partner or by themselves, so I can see how they do as a class.

Thinking About Math
Student Name:
Date:

Too Easy	Too Hard	Just Right

The Big Picture

The examples in this chapter illustrate how instruction is changing as we involve students in the assessment process. When teachers involve students in the process of linking to prior knowledge, describing success, setting criteria, giving feedback, and assessing their own learning, they are teaching students how to learn as well as teaching them what they need to know and be able to do.

Building Your Inukshuk

1. Think about assessment in your classroom. How does it guide instruction? How do you involve students in the process? What do you do that is the same as the ideas you have read in this chapter? What is different? Record your thoughts.

2. Collect some evidence or ideas from your classroom or school to share with a learning circle. Listen to each other talk about classroom assessment experiences that support student learning. What lessons are there for you and for your learning group members?

Chapter 7

Collecting, Organizing, and Presenting Evidence

The student knows more than the teacher about what and how he has learned—even if he knows less about what was taught.

Peter Elbow

Collecting, organizing, and presenting evidence of learning used to be the teacher's responsibility alone. If students are to be involved in their learning, then they must also be involved in this crucial aspect. Part of learning is recognizing when you've succeeded. You know you've succeeded when you see the evidence. Learners need to collect and organize their evidence so they know they are learning. They also need to present their evidence so others will also know they are learning. That's what it means to be accountable.

To have all the evidence we need for balanced and fair assessment, teachers can't just review work once, record the mark, and then file or send the work home. Instead, we need to involve students in gathering and creating comprehensive collections of evidence—products, self-assessments, and recorded observations. The student's collection of evidence becomes a visual history of her or his learning over time. Both the collection itself and the process of making it are valuable in several ways.

- Students can use their collections to show teachers and parents what they know and what they need to learn. This process helps students better understand their own learning and their progress.

- Students' collections of evidence help improve the quality and specificity of communications between teachers, students, and parents. Showing collections of evidence to parents provides the information they need to be partners in the assessment process and helps demystify the learning process.

- Creating collections of evidence helps students to learn and practise organizational skills, to take pride in their work, and to learn about themselves as learners. When students learn to present themselves and their learning to others, they develop skills that prepare them for life.

- Because collections of evidence help students and parents see the learning for themselves, they are a rich resource for reporting. They enlarge the view of what has been learned, provide a window into student thinking, and give a multi-dimensional view of the student as a learner. The more extensive the collection of evidence, the better view it gives of the learner. A range of evidence collected over time and across different tasks increases the validity and reliability of the assessment and evaluation for everyone.

Making the Process Work

There are four keys to ensuring that collecting and organizing evidence supports student learning in your classroom:

- Keep the process simple.
- Involve students in being responsible for the evidence.
- Include more than written work as evidence.
- Help parents and students understand why the evidence is important.

Keep the Process Simple

Simplicity is the key to a system that will take the least amount of time to maintain. I believe the only complexity we can afford to invite into our classrooms is our students (and they are more complex day-by-day). Our assessment processes, including collecting evidence, need to be practical and possible, and they need to support learning in powerful ways.

Here are some points to keep in mind when designing a process:

- Help students understand why they are keeping track of their evidence.
- Explain who is going to see the evidence.
- Work with students to design a simple system that they can use (e.g., folders or magazine files).
- Provide students with time to store their evidence.

How you choose to have students involved in collecting and organizing evidence depends on many factors, such as physical space, the age of your students, and whether you teach one class or several. To keep the evidence safe, have a system such as folders, boxes, or bins. Provide time for students to collect evidence and be organized. Once a system to organize the physical evidence is in place, plan to give students time to add to the collection of evidence regularly. Have students keep as much evidence as they can—you never know what might be important later. In addition to students' collections, teachers still need to collect their own observation notes and evidence they will need later for evaluation.

There is a range of ways teachers and students choose to collect, organize, and present evidence. Here are just a few examples.

- Ms. M's primary students collect their work in notebooks, personal magazine file boxes, and progress portfolios.

- Mr. S's intermediate students have file drawers in which they store loose papers, their binders, and portfolios that they select entries for each Friday. They are just in the process of setting up their class Web site so parents can visit and view student work.

- Ms. R's Grade 8 students have progress portfolios, back-and-forth work folders, and fat folders. The fat folders are stored in plastic crates near her desk.

- Ms. G's Grade 9 students have writing folders, notebooks, and folders from which they select work to show how they are learning over time.

- Mr. C teaches university students. His students keep whatever they need to have on hand when they meet with him at the end of the semester to explain their learning. Their decision-making process is guided by the detailed description of what kind of evidence is needed. He also involves students in developing criteria for each assignment and encourages them to resubmit assignments up until the end of the course.

Involve Students

Students need to be accountable for their learning—it helps us and it helps them. When students keep track of the evidence, they have more opportunities to figure out whether they are on track with their learning. It is the teacher's job to show them how to do it well.

Involve students in planning for success by asking them what they think they need in order to be organized and to monitor their progress. Sometimes students just file the evidence and sort it later. Some teachers arrange time so students can record what the evidence is and what they want the viewer to notice. When students explain the learning the evidence represents, they learn more about themselves as learners.

When I chose to include this example of my writing in my portfolio I remembered that . . .

Fiction
- has a good story
- uses interesting language
- has a beginning, a middle, and an end
- uses a variety of sentences, both simple and complex

Non-fiction
- gives information
- groups information under main headings
- has a table of contents
- has diagrams or pictures to give additional information

I also know that it is important that my work is neat and that it has been edited for spelling and sentence structure.

The piece of work I have chosen is . . .

It shows . . .

I want you to notice . . .

Please give me one compliment and ask me one question after you read my selection.

I put this in my portfolio on _____ _____
                                        (date)   (signature)

From Davies, et al., *Together is Better*, 68.

Research shows that the brain recalls pictures faster and with more accuracy than it recalls words.

(Sprenger 1998; Politano and Paquin 2000)

Later, when parents view the evidence, read the notes students have made, and listen to students talk about their learning, they are more informed.

Include More Than Written Work

As students are increasingly asked to represent what they know in a variety of ways, the evidence starts to expand beyond being primarily "paper and pencil." Some kinds of evidence, such as a play or the construction of a Hudson's Bay trading post, can't remain in your classroom unless represented in some other form. Work with students to figure out how the evidence can be recorded in another way, such as photographs, videotape, audiotape, or posted at a Web site. Records such as these help capture the learning that otherwise might be forgotten.

Help Parents and Students to Value the Evidence

Building collections of evidence usually means that only some student work goes home, while the rest stays at school so that it is on hand for review and discussion. Sometimes students take home weekly files of work and then bring them back after parents have viewed them. Sometimes students store almost all evidence at school. Parents who may be used to getting samples of student work brought home on a weekly or daily basis may wonder if any learning is taking place at all. Take time to explain. You might have students write notes explaining why the evidence is

This piece is an example of . . .

I want you to notice . . .

Date _____ _____
                                      (signature)

From Davies, et al., *Together is Better*, 94.

important and where it can be viewed. Once school has been in session for a while, the class might invite parents to an afternoon open house to view the evidence; students might prepare for and then conduct an at-home conference with their parents; or students might give parents a tour of the class Web site.

As you increase the amount of descriptive feedback and decrease the amount of evaluative feedback, you may not be marking or grading work in ways parents expect. Let parents know you are continuing to assess student work. Explain that you may choose to not respond to student work with a mark or grade, but that you will be assessing all student work. A note such as the one shown here helps to explain your approach and alleviate parent concerns.

Dear Parents:

As you look through your child's work, please notice, as I have, the areas he/she has had success with and the things she/he needs to improve upon.

While I have assessed all the work in this collection, I have chosen to place a mark or write a note about only some of the work.

If you have any questions about your child's learning, I would be pleased to discuss it with you. Please call me to arrange a time to talk.

Best wishes,

Mr. Taylor

P.S. Sarah, it was a pleasure to see you last week. Jill was thrilled with your note. We are having a second-hand book sale next month. Could you spare some time to help us organize it?

Portfolios

When students present their work to others, they share all or part of the evidence they have been collecting. Collections of evidence can include any evidence the student has created, such as notebooks, projects, assignments, computer storage disks or CDs, videotapes or audiotapes, or written tests. A collection of evidence with a focused purpose is called a portfolio. Portfolios can have a variety of purposes.

When students select evidence for a portfolio, they explain why the piece of evidence was included. When the audience (parents, peers, teachers) knows why evidence has been included, they are more likely to understand the learning it represents. One way to do this is to include a self-assessment that explains the significance of the piece or use categories such as "Best Work" or "Most Improved." Notes such as these are attached to student work to guide the viewer and explain the significance of the work.

> The hardest word I know how to spell is Wednesday.
>
> It is hard because you can't hear the d.
>
> The most interesting word I know how to spell is humongous.
>
> It is interesting because we couldn't find it in the dictionary.
>
> I'd like you to know I like getting to make the list to take
>
> home to do with my mom and some of them are my words.
>
> signed: Justin

From Smith and Davies, *Wordsmithing*, 88.

Many portfolios include a summary page on which students record their strengths and the areas needing improvement, and propose one or two goals for the upcoming term. Students also include a response form for the audience. This completed response form later becomes part of the portfolio.

Selecting with a Purpose

Teachers decide with students who is going to see the evidence and what the audience would most appreciate knowing about student learning. The purpose and audience gives a focus for sorting the evidence. This allows the portfolio to send a powerful message about the learner and the learning.

Progress Portfolios

A progress portfolio provides snapshots of learning over time. When the audience reviews the progress portfolio, the progress or growth in learning speaks for itself. Similar to asking a child to stand against the door frame or chart to show his or her growth in height, teachers ask students to select pieces of work to show how much they have grown in a particular area or in several areas since the last measure.

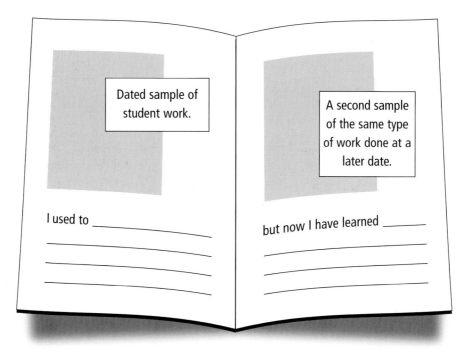

Dated sample of student work.

A second sample of the same type of work done at a later date.

I used to _____

but now I have learned _____

Process Portfolios

Process portfolios show the learning process. The purpose is to show learning taking place over time—all the stages, not just key points. Students collect evidence of different stages in their work such as pre-writing, drafts, and published work, or samples showing development in math each week.

Best-Work Portfolios

Best-work or showcase portfolios show student learning by highlighting accomplishments. Similar to preparing for a job interview, students select evidence to best show their accomplishments. After identifying strengths and achievements, students highlight one or two areas needing improvement and identify their goals.

Learning Goals Portfolios

A learning goals portfolio is organized to show how well students are able to meet the learning goals expected for a particular grade level and subject area. It includes a clear statement of each goal, pieces of work the student selected, and an explanation of how each piece of work addresses the goal.

Taking the Time

It takes time to introduce and support students as they assume a larger role in collecting their own assessment evidence. It is time worth taking because students have an opportunity to become more responsible and involved in their own learning and, as a result, learn more. It is also time worth taking because students know their audience (their parents and family members as well as their teacher) and what evidence their audience needs to help them understand and appreciate the learning.

As teachers we decide the balance of teacher work and student involvement that is comfortable for us—there is no one right way. The balance between teacher work and student work will vary from year to year. As you make your choices, remember that the person who is working the hardest is learning the most.

Building Your Inukshuk

1. Ask your colleagues how their students are involved in organizing and collecting evidence. Listen for ideas that might help you, as well as ways that they involve students to make it easier. Record the ideas.

2. Think about the evidence your students will produce and what you think the audience needs to learn about as they review it. Do you want them to see the progress or the process, or do you want to highlight the successes? Record your thoughts and decide on one thing you want to begin doing differently.

3. In a group of teachers, ask each person to talk about how she or he organizes evidence, highlighting how students are involved to make the teacher's job easier and build ownership. Ask a recorder to make a list of all ideas. Listen to the range of what works.

4. Ask each group member how his or her students organize the evidence. What is the purpose? Who is the major audience? Listen for ideas that might help you as you plan. When you have listened to each member of the group, do a ten-minute journal reflection on the power of involving students in collecting and organizing evidence of their own learning.

Chapter ⑧

Communicating About Learning

> . . . we can tell a little more of the truth. In doing so, it turns out that we can avoid pretending that a student's whole performance or intelligence can be summed up in one number.
>
> Peter Elbow

In the past, informal communications—such as conversations by the boot racks or on the lanai, notes home, a conversation in the local market, or a telephone call—helped build partnerships between home and school. Casual communications kept students, their families, and teachers moving along in similar directions.

Increasingly, as families become busier, daily life gets more complex, and the information glut overwhelms even the most organized of us, there is less time to be informed—even though many parents want to know more. The challenge is also increasing as our communities become more diverse and values seem so different. Sometimes we might wonder if there is a common meeting place. But there is. The place where families, schools, and teachers come together is in caring about the student. We all want the best for each student, even though we may express it in different ways.

Successful Communications

One solution to the challenge of finding ways to communicate can be found in involving students. When students communicate with others about their learning, they learn about what they have learned, what they need to learn, and what kind of support may be available to them. They receive feedback and recognition from themselves and from others that guides and supports their learning. The process of preparing and presenting gives students an opportunity to construct their understanding and to help others make meaning of their learning. This is all part of learning to self-monitor—an essential skill for self-directed, independent, lifelong learners.

Having parents and others watch demonstrations of learning or attend student-parent conferences increases their appreciation of their son or daughter as a learner, his or her level of skill development, the breadth of the classroom and school curriculum, and the efforts needed on everyone's behalf to make learning possible. When the audience is invited to respond, they acknowledge and support the learning while giving students valuable feedback.

There are three parts to successful communication about learning:

- students show or demonstrate their learning
- parents respond to students
- the teacher invites feedback to improve the process

Students Show or Demonstrate Their Learning

When students are involved in preparing and organizing the communication for a specific audience, the message is more likely to be understood. This is partly because students themselves have a good idea about the best way to communicate with different audiences. Audiences may be parents, family members, family friends, students in another class, or members of the community. Having a specific audience helps communications about student learning be more focused, purposeful, and more likely to inform.

Teachers develop ways to communicate about student learning that work for them, for students, for parents, and for the school community. For example, one class invited their parents for an open house, and the students explained their classroom program using Readers' Theatre (Nye 1999).

When students are involved, the teacher's role changes from doing the communicating to guiding the process and organizing students to show or demonstrate their learning. Some possibilities are student-generated newsletters, student self-assessments and work samples, demonstrations of learning at home or at school, and student-parent conferences.

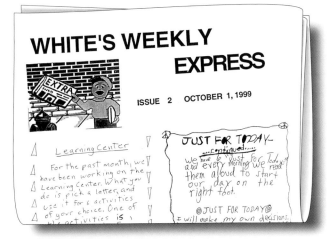

Adapted by Dolores White from Politano and Davies, *Multi-Age and More*, 114.

Student-Generated Newsletters

Student-generated newsletters provide parents with information about the classroom program as well as student learning. Teachers ask students to work individually or in small groups to take responsibility for communicating about the learning taking place day by day in classrooms. Creating the newsletter is a valuable experience for students. It gives a real purpose and audience for their efforts, and it requires them to articulate their learning and make sense of it for others.

Self-Assessments and Work Samples

Teachers ask students to think about and reflect on their work because it helps students learn. When teachers ask students to share these self-assessments with their parents, the self-assessments become a valuable way to communicate about learning. Shared self-assessments with samples of student work sent home for parent review might include two math work samples showing progress; a portfolio showing best work; a photograph of the student at work, with an explanation of what the student is learning about; or a videotape that records students performing. Student self-assessments and accompanying work samples are selected to show a range that allows parents to see the breadth of classroom work beyond "paper and pencil" evidence.

Such communications keep parents up to date and help students realize that there is an audience for their work. Completed response forms give students feedback and help teachers understand what the audience values.

Picture This!

This weekend for outdoor education I went surf kayaking in the ocean. It was really hard at first, but when I figured out how to roll back up when I flipped, it made the weekend a lot more fun. That also helped me to keep out of the cold water so I could stay out longer.

P.S. My friend Alison Kakish took this photo.

Adapted from Gregory, Cameron, and Davies, *Conferencing and Reporting,* In Press.

Demonstrations of Learning at Home or at School

Sometimes an effective way for students to show parents what they've learned is through demonstrations that take place at home or at school. Students may take home a math game, the materials for a science experiment, a musical instrument, a videotaped performance, or a book to read aloud and invite parents to respond.

Sometimes a classroom teacher will organize a demonstration of learning to take place at school. This may include a family subject-focused activity such as a Math Night where children teach parents math games in the library, a student-parent conference where students show parents and extended family members their portfolios or collections of school work, or a science laboratory experiment conducted by students for parents in the lab.

Most schools involve students in demonstrating their learning in some way during the year. Schools plan events such as seasonal music concerts, drama performances, track meets, fine arts open houses, and formal debates. Teachers are learning ways to invite feedback from the audience during these events. This includes involving students in welcoming audience members by describing the learning they are about to see, and having students present and then invite the audience to respond. Responses give students feedback on and acknowledgment for what they have learned.

Student-Parent Conferences

Student-parent conferences are a time for students to share their learning with their parents. Teachers help students prepare to conduct student-parent conferences, whether they are going to take place at home or at school. Students have an agenda; organized evidence of their learning, such as their notebooks, projects, or portfolios; and something to demonstrate, such as a book to read aloud. The discussion is led by the student as evidence of learning is shared. At the end of the conference, students ask their parents to give them feedback on a prepared response form. Sometimes parents and students will also set goals for future learning.

> ### Congratulations, Everyone
>
> We saw you at the Sharing Assembly and would like you to know
>
> - We enjoyed your poetry reading
> - It made us laugh
> - We could hear you at the back
>
> Shane's Mom and Dad

Adapted from Cameron, et al., *Recognition Without Rewards*, 27.

Dear Guests:

Welcome to our class. Please let your son or daughter be your guide. She or he will teach you about some of the things we do at school.

1. With your guide, visit the learning centres in our classroom. Ask lots of questions. Your guide will invite you to participate in some of the activities at each centre.

2. Your guide is also ready to show you:

   • a portfolio and an Assessment Centre collection
   • notebooks
   • a favourite library book
   • a favourite computer program
   • the book fair in the library

3. When you are finished your tour, your guide will ask you to complete a response form. This form will ask you to give two compliments and one wish for your child and his or her learning.

When conferences are held at school, there are many different formats. One teacher might ask five students to sign up for each 30-minute period. During that time, they conduct their student-parent conference, and the teacher meets with each family for a few minutes. Another teacher might have as many student-parent conferences as there is space and be available to respond to questions. The choices teachers make concerning the number of student-parent conferences to schedule at one time depends on their purpose, students' needs, their family's needs, and the teacher's comfort level with the process.

The following example describes how one school used a "learning centres" or "stations" approach for student-parent conferences. These conferences were held about two weeks before the end of term.

The number of centres depended on the class and ranged in number from 4 to 12. Students invited their families, and together they moved from centre to centre. Most teachers encouraged families to sign up for one of the two hours scheduled for this event. This helped foster an "open house" atmosphere in which families could spend up to an hour visiting the centres.

At each centre, parents participated in an activity that the student was currently doing in the class. This included activities such as building complex patterns using pattern blocks, solving equations, using frames to write poems, reading a book, taking apart something in the Deconstruction Centre, or looking through the student's portfolio in the Assessment Centre.

Teachers posted signs for families that explained some of the key ways the activities related to the curriculum goals and suggested some questions families might want to ask their children. Students were ready to explain what the centre was about, show other work related to the centre activities, and answer their families' questions. As they arrived, guests were given a note that acted as an agenda explaining what would happen during the visit.

Student-parent conferences are a valuable part of communicating about learning, but they do not replace conferences that include the teacher. When evaluation is involved, it is important to have the person who is responsible for evaluation (the teacher) present. This is best done through student-parent-teacher conferences, which are described in Chapter 9.

Dear Parents:

It is helpful for your child to have your comments about his or her learning at the conclusion of Math Night. When we know we have done something right, we feel good about ourselves. We accept challenges more readily and enthusiastically, and learning becomes easier. In the space below, please give your son or daughter two specific compliments and one wish.

Thank you.

> Two compliments for: Kayla
>
> • The way you are learning to do math and that you love it.
> • That you are always happy after school, so you are obviously loving it!
>
> One Wish:
>
> That you continue to love learning and that you aren't afraid to ask questions, whatever they are!
>
> From: Mommy and Daddy

Adapted from Davies, et al., *Together Is Better*, 53.

Parents Respond

Every time students share their learning with parents or another audience, it is a good idea to invite parents (or the audience) to respond. When parents are invited to respond to their children's learning, they deepen their relationship with their child, students understand that their learning is valued, and everyone understands the learning more. This response can be as simple as a form that asks the reader to notice something positive about the learning as well as ask a question, give some advice, or suggest an improvement.

The Teacher Invites Feedback

Whenever we invite students to communicate about their learning to others, it is important to follow up to find out whether it was successful for students and for the audience. Even with the best of intentions, mistakes are made. We need to know what is working and what is not so that we can continue to learn ourselves.

Math Night Survey

Dear Students and Parents:

Feedback is essential for learning—we need to know what worked (do more of) and what did not (do less of). Please help us learn to do a better job of student-parent conferences by responding to this survey. You do not need to sign it, but please send the completed survey back to the school secretary so it can be put in the collection box in the school's main office.

Thank you!

What are two compliments you have about Math Night?

> We could see the growth in our son's work and confidence. We were pleased to see the variety of his math work. I especially liked that he felt in control. He was proud to show his achievements. I also liked his "agenda." He had a specific order to show his work. He was well prepared.

Is there anything you'd like to see or do next time we have a Math Night?

> It is important for our son to show his learning, but we also want to know what you think. Will you be a part of our report card conference next month? Last year the teacher had lots of conferences at one time, and we didn't get a chance to find out what she thought.

Adapted from Politano and Davies, *Multi-Age and More*, 107.

Ask students and parents what worked and what did not. Be careful what you ask for. Asking for one or two compliments and one piece of advice is enough. Consider keeping surveys anonymous so students and parents will feel more comfortable expressing their thoughts. Let students and parents know what was said by posting a summary of the comments on the class Web site, or ask students to include it in the next class newsletter home.

Finding Your Way

When we involve students in communicating about their learning, we are inviting them and their parents to have thoughtful conversations with us and with each other about learning. There is no one *right* or *best* way to do this. Select the method or combination of methods that work for you, your students, and their families in your school community.

1. Record your ideas about your current communication practices. Reflect on the following:

    - How do you currently communicate with parents about student learning?
    - How are students involved? How are parents invited to be involved and to respond?
    - How could you increase student involvement in the communication process?
    - What kind of balance of teacher, parent, and student input do you think would be best?
    - Do your students need to be doing more? How could you simplify the communication process?

2. In a group, share ideas about what works. Gather samples. Talk through simple and effective ways to increase student involvement.

3. Consider how the responsibility for communicating student learning could be shared with others—colleagues, students, parents. Create a personal plan.

Chapter 9

Evaluating and Reporting

> We must constantly remind ourselves that the ultimate purpose of evaluation is to enable students to evaluate themselves.
>
> Arthur Costa

Evaluation and reporting are at the point in the classroom assessment cycle when the learning pauses, the evidence is organized and evaluated by comparing it to the description of learning, and then the results of the evaluation are shared in a report card. The foundation for evaluating and reporting is put in place when the teacher develops the descriptions of learning (Chapter 3), describes what success looks like for students (Chapter 4), and thinks through the evidence that will be needed (Chapter 5). When it is time to evaluate, teachers revisit those same descriptions, review the evidence, make their evaluations, check them out with students and their parents, and report using the required format. Evaluating and reporting are straightforward last steps in an assessment process that begins much earlier.

Working Together

Evaluating and reporting address four questions:

- What does the student know and what is she or he able to do?
- What areas require further attention or development?
- In what ways can the student's learning be supported?
- How is the student progressing in relation to the standards of development for students in a similar age range?

Teachers, students, and parents each have a role in the evaluating and reporting process. Students do the learning, create the evidence, and organize it, summarizing their strengths, needs, and plans. They present the evidence to account for their learning and listen to feedback. They are then involved in setting goals for future learning.

Parents participate by listening, watching, asking questions, and making sense of the evidence. They interpret the evidence and self-assessments students present and the commentary the teacher gives. They add to this their own observations of their son or daughter as a learner.

Teachers, because it is their professional responsibility, are the final arbitrators and evaluators of the work. They assist students to communicate their learning to parents, and they make themselves available to talk about how they have evaluated the student's work as well as to discuss ways to support student learning.

A Subjective Process

The evaluating and reporting process includes evaluating the evidence, involving students and parents in reviewing the evidence, summarizing strengths and areas needing improvement, and finalizing the report.

Teachers' professional lives might be more pleasant if evaluating and reporting could be tidy and objective, but they aren't. Evaluation is inherently subjective. The more evidence collected and the longer the period of time over which it is collected, the more confidence everyone can have in the evaluation.

We also increase the validity of our evaluation by triangulating the evidence and by involving students and their parents in reviewing the evidence and affirming whether or not the evaluation makes sense.

Evaluating the Evidence

Evaluation is a process of looking at all the evidence, comparing it to the description, and asking "Did this student learn what was to be learned? How well?" When we evaluate, we determine the worth or value of the evidence—we appraise it with respect to excellence or merit. Simply totalling the marks or grades in our record book means that important evidence may not be considered. To evaluate well, we should look at *all* the evidence—observations, products, and conversations. We can then use this evidence to determine whether the student has met the widely held expectations for his or her age.

In evaluation, teachers must be especially careful when working with numbers (scores) from performance scales and rubrics. If feedback is evaluated and recorded as numbers, those numbers can't be totalled and averaged with other kinds of numbers. It is like adding mangoes, potatoes, apples, and trees—they are all different things. You may be able to create a formula to do it, but what you get does not make mathematical sense. Rather than totalling numbers that can't really be totalled, consider *matching* evidence to the description of learning.

When we evaluate, triangulation of evidence—looking at evidence from three different sources—is essential because it puts single pieces of evidence into context. Just as a judge in a court of law has to examine all the evidence in light of the laws, when we evaluate, we look at all the evidence in light of the description of learning. We must consider all the evidence—the assessments students have made, our observations, criteria-based assessments attached to projects or assignments, performance grids, and marks from projects and tests.

Reporting

Reporting used to be a special event that happened only at set times in a year. Now it is an ongoing process that involves students, parents, and teachers in examining and making sense of a student's learning. Every time students speak with their parents about learning, they are reporting. They are reporting when they take home samples of their work and talk with parents about them. They are reporting when they invite parents to a portfolio afternoon to look at the work or to participate in a student-parent-teacher conference.

Formal evaluating and reporting is usually required by legislation or policy and is a process of looking at the evidence, having conversations and conferences about what the evidence means, and keeping a written record of the conversation for the permanent file or record.

Increasingly, teachers are involving students in the conferencing and reporting process and inviting them and their parents to be a part of student-parent-teacher conferences. The purpose of these conferences is to look at the evidence, highlight strengths, discuss areas needing improvement, and set goals. They take place during the reporting period so parents can look at all the evidence.

Here is how two teachers use the process.

➤ Mrs. H has created an observation chart for her early primary class that details what she needs to be teaching and observing in different subject areas. When reporting time nears, she has students organize their evidence, collect samples for their progress portfolios, and do self-reports. In their self-reports students record their strengths, areas needing improvement, and goals. They rehearse what they are going to say to their parents. Parents respond with two compliments and one wish. Mrs. H summarizes the evidence on an observation chart, writes a draft report, and shares both her report and the child's self-report with the parents.

October Goal: To get better at reading

December Progress:
I W13D aA M2AJ81E
I read the message boad.

Feb. 24 E5 deep
b.5 (Easy Reader books)

Sample from Hanahau'oli Elementary School, Hawaii.

During their student-parent-teacher conference, they review the strengths and areas needing improvement. The student shares the progress portfolio, telling what she or he learned. Mrs. H shares the draft report. Together, student, parents, and teacher set goals and discuss support for learning. Once the conference is over, Mrs. H finalizes the one-page narrative report that summarizes the conference discussion. She reads it to the student, checking to see if anything is missing or if something is incorrect. One copy is filed and one is sent home with an invitation for parents to get in touch if there are any remaining questions or concerns.

➤ Mr. M has his Grade 7 students organize their evidence, collect samples for their progress portfolios, and do self-reports. In their self-reports, students record their strengths, areas needing improvement, and goals. Mr. M does a draft report and shares both his report and the child's self-report with the parents. Parents are also invited to review the evidence and do a report for their child, highlighting strengths, areas needing improvement, and possible goals. During their student-parent-teacher conference they review the strengths and areas needing improvement, and set goals. Once the conference is over and the written report is finalized, one copy is filed and one sent home. As part of the follow-up, Mr. M debriefs the process with students, and parents are invited to request a separate parent-teacher conference should they need one. Mr. M gets very few requests for follow-up conferences.

"I think the conference was good because it gives my parents a really good idea of how I am doing at school."

"I liked it because my mom got to have a chance to tell my teacher what I am good at. Also I like it because I could tell both my mom and my teacher what I need to have help on and more stuff."

"I really liked the conference because I got to show my mom lots of stuff that I was doing and because me and Ms. R made a goal for me, which was to speak up more and be part of the conversation. And I think I'm doing really good at that."

Involving Students

Teachers are seeing the benefits of showing students their reports before they go home and of asking questions such as "Does this make sense? Does it reflect your learning? Is it fair? Am I missing anything?" This increases the validity of our evaluation because we add the student's perspective to the range of information we have to work with. Once students understand their reports, they are also more likely to be able to help explain them to their parents.

"I think it helps the child to know that all parties are working together to help them with their progress."

"With the three-way conferencing I seem to get a better feel of where my child's strengths and weaknesses are and suggestions on how to work with him. I get a better idea of what is expected of a student of that level."

"I think the conferences are an essential part of reporting. A report card cannot possibly provide all the information available. The opportunity for the student is invaluable."

Involving Parents

Keeping track of how their children are doing at school is a challenge for most parents. In a student-and-parent-involved evaluation and reporting process, parents have an opportunity to be involved in reviewing the evidence, listening to their son or daughter talk about their strengths and areas needing improvement, helping to set goals for future learning, and identifying plans for supporting the student's learning.

In addition to listening to their child and looking at the evidence,

"During a student-parent-teacher conference . . . you can show parents what the students can do and discuss this with them. You can find out what individual parents want to know about their child in terms of assessment and reporting. This means less work, as I hold the conference before I write the report card . . . there are no surprises for the parents and I have an individual report tailored for each student."

"For middle school students there is always a genuine sense of closure and satisfaction about the whole process. There are no loose ends. Student-parent-teacher conferences are the best way to instill a sense of student responsibility for their own learning."

"When the five-year-olds in our program share their progress portfolios with their families in three-way conferences by showing the work they've done on their goals, it's an amazing learning, teaching, and assessment opportunity all rolled into one."

parents need opportunities to listen to the teacher and to have the teacher respond to any questions they may have about their child's learning. After the conference and reporting process is completed, teachers can invite parents to get in touch about any remaining concerns or questions that have arisen about their son's or daughter's learning. To invite parents to give feedback about the process, teachers send home a follow-up survey.

Compensating for the Compulsory

For many teachers and administrators, the need to work within the reporting guidelines and support student learning seem contradictory. Bibby and Posterski (1992), in their book, *Teen Trends: A Nation in Motion*, use the phrase "compensating for the compulsory" to describe those things we can try to do to live within the rules while making things work better.

One area where teachers find themselves compensating for the compulsory is letter grades. The body of research concerning letter grades is summarized well by Kohn (1999). He says that traditional grades are likely to lead to three separate results: less impressive learning, less interest in learning, and less desire to do challenging learning. He recommends that if you do have to give letter grades, you give as few as possible. Letter grades get in the way of student learning—the best teachers can do is "compensate for the compulsory."

Because letter grades and other symbols give many students the message that they are not able learners, they may become less able.

(Jensen 1998; Sylwester 1995; Seagoe 1970; Smith 1986)

As teachers we can't rewrite the regulations that govern reporting, but we can look at them and think about how best to work within them on behalf of student learning. Where jurisdictions still require teachers to report using letter grades, a growing number of teachers are talking with students about what counts in their learning, sharing information about how a letter grade is arrived at before the end of the term, and involving them in the conferencing and reporting process. This doesn't make letter grades right, it just makes them a little better. Here is how two teachers report using letter grades.

> Letter grades and other symbols have a negative effect on learning for all students except those of high ability and high achievement who feel letter grades and other symbols are important.
>
> (Butler 1987, 1988; Butterworth and Michael 1975; Calkins 1991; Curwin 1978; Harter 1978; Kyle 1992; Natriello 1984)

➤ Ms. C teaches a fifth-year course to teachers finishing the last year of their degree. She provides students with the course outcomes and a description of each letter grade. She sets criteria for each assignment with them. At the end of the course there is a student-teacher conference so students can present to her their evidence of learning in relation to the course outcomes. She reviews all the evidence and uses the description of letter grades to determine students' final grades in the course.

➤ Ms. G teaches Grade 9 English. She has identified what she needs students to learn, the evidence that she will be collecting, and, since she is required to give students letter grades of A, B, C+, or C, she has described what the learning and evidence look like at each level. Earlier in the term she shared these descriptions with students and their parents. Prior to reporting, students organize their evidence into portfolios and review it to ensure that it includes everything they need to substantiate their grades. Ms. G reviews the student evidence, including the marks she recorded and her own observations, and evaluates the learning. The student is assigned the letter grade that matches the evidence. Each student receives a copy of Ms. G's evaluation. Parents are invited to come to the school for a student-parent conference to view the evidence before the reports are prepared. Once the reports are sent home, parents are invited to call Ms. G if they need to ask any questions about the evaluation or the report or to sign up for a conference.

Putting It Together

Description of Learning
Grade 9 English

- Reads a great ⌐
  style and form,

- Uses a wide va
  different genre
  inferential leve

- Responds with
  powerful conne
  others, and to ⌐

- Writes effectiv⌐
  appropriate to

- Consistently fo
  punctuation, ar

- Works producti

Triangulation of Evidence
Grade 9 English

Ob⌐

- r⌐
- s⌐
  w
- li⌐

Conversatior

- student conf⌐
- self-assessm⌐

Criteria for Evaluation
Grade 9 English

Description of an A—*Outstanding* Level of Performance

These students:

- consistently write high-quality entries in their response notebooks (i.e., consistently meet the criteria)
- select reading material that is appropriate for their accomplished level of reading skill
- are self-directed readers (evidence shown in the number and quality of reader responses which have been done both in class time and at home)
- consistently submit high-quality second drafts that show evidence of thoughtful revision and editing
- use their writing source books to practise different forms and formats of writing as well as to note ideas, opinions, and so on
- are self-directed writers (evidence shown in the number and variety of first drafts in their writing source books that have been done both in class and at home)
- consistently achieve high test scores (i.e., 86 percent and above)
- consistently demonstrate their ability to ask and answer thoughtful questions and to analyze literature skilfully
- consistently and independently complete all assignments to a high level of quality (consistently meet the criteria)

Adapted from Gregory, Cameron, and Davies,
Conferencing and Reporting, In Press.

Common Elements

Of course, you will need to figure out what processes of evaluation and reporting will work for you, your students, and their parents, given the situation you are in. When you're thinking it through, you might want to consider some of the processes presented in the examples in this chapter. These teachers:

- worked within the legal requirements for reporting in their schools and districts
- developed a description of what learning looks like
- involved students in the classroom assessment process
- collected samples of growth over time
- involved students in collecting and organizing the evidence
- spent time examining the evidence and doing their own evaluation
- checked with students to ensure the teacher's evaluation of their work made sense
- asked parents to review the evidence and invited them to also do a "report" from their perspective
- met with each student and her or his parents to discuss strengths, areas needing improvement, and goals
- told parents whether or not their child's learning was in the "safety zone" or whether intervention was needed
- finalized the report after conversation with participants
- put a copy in the student's permanent file

When you make your plans for evaluating and reporting, take the time to be sure you know what rules and regulations govern evaluation and reporting in your school. Ask at the district or province/state level. Don't be easily satisfied by hearing someone else's interpretation of the rules. Become an expert on exactly what you are responsible for so that you can figure out the best way to use the evaluation and reporting process to support student learning.

It is well worth taking this time. As Mary Anne Drummond (1994) explains, "The process of assessing children's learning—by looking closely at it and striving to understand it—is the only certain safeguard against children's failure, the only certain guarantee of children's progress and development."

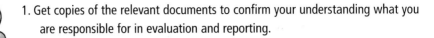

1. Get copies of the relevant documents to confirm your understanding what you are responsible for in evaluation and reporting.

2. Write about any differences you notice between what you know the requirements to be after some investigation and what you used to think they were. If you see differences, what steps could you take to improve your evaluation process? Especially think of ways you could involve students and parents more.

3. In a group, take turns explaining the way you evaluate. As you listen to each other, think about what parts make sense and what parts do not. List the perceived barriers to evaluating in better ways. Share your understanding of the rules and regulations. What kinds of freedom do you currently have? What kinds of freedom might you be able to have?

4. Think about what might help you streamline the process you use and make it more powerful. Choose one thing to work on to improve your evaluation process. Create a plan. Find a friend or colleague to support you as you learn.

Chapter 🔟

Final Thoughts

Certainty stunts thought, in ourselves and others . . . . Thought flourishes as questions are asked, not as answers are found.

Frank Smith

As we begin this new millennium, we are awash in the problems arising from yesterday's solutions. As humans we search to find the simple within the complex. It is elusive, so when we find it, we tend to hold it tight. More than a hundred years ago there was a problem—how to rank, sort, and group learners for their roles in the industrial world. Assessment became a large part of the solution. Now, even though the problem has changed, many of the old solutions continue to be used. As Willard Daggart (1991) said, "We are speeding towards the future while looking in the rear-view mirror." Not safe. Our past, while informing our actions, should not dictate them.

As we discover more about the challenges we face, we are seeking to ensure that each person leaves his or her family, community, and school prepared to be a independent, self-directed, lifelong learner—a person who is prepared to have many careers over a lifetime. Doing more of what we used to think worked—such as more testing, more failure and retention, higher standards, more rewards, greater punishments, and tighter control over students and their learning—is hurting, not helping (Barlow and Robertson 1994; Biddle and Berliner 1998; Natriello 1984; Shepard and Smith 1986; Rothman 1995).

Making classroom assessment work means reframing the conversation from one about ranking and sorting students to one about assessing learning in the context of our students' futures. It means talking with and listening to learners, their parents, and the community about learning and about assessment. It means involving students and parents, giving choices, and sharing control. When it comes to classroom assessment, solutions can only be found in thoughtful, informed conversation as we work together on behalf of students and their learning.

As we explore and discover new ideas, we also need to be cautious in our enthusiasm to share what we learn. When we find something that works for us, we need to refrain from thinking it is the answer and packaging it for others. Just like the difference between sheet music, which makes everyone play the same tune no matter what kind of music they like, and a collection of notes, which allows everyone to find a tune that works for them, the "right answer" limits others unnecessarily. Teachers, students, and parents need the flexibility to address individual needs as well as provide for choice and diversity in order to support each student's learning. Classroom assessment that supports student learning and informs parents guides us— just like an Inukshuk.

Acknowledgments

When I was 20 years old, I began teaching in Yellowknife, Northwest Territories. My colleagues welcomed me into the profession, freely shared their knowledge of learning and teaching, and guided me through my first years as a teacher. I came to better understand the gift they had given me when I saw my first Inukshuk while travelling in the Arctic. As I imagined what it must be like to find your way with little to guide you, I appreciated the enormity of what they had done.

Thank you to my circle of friends and colleagues. When we share ideas, teach with our stories, and support each other's learning, we all learn and are better able to support the learners with whom we each work.

Editing your own writing is, at a certain point, impossible and best done by a professional. My thanks to three professionals—Annalee Greenberg, who said this was an important book, when I thought it was maybe a good article; Sharon Sterling, who, with her talented editing and thoughtful queries, helped me find the book within the manuscript; and Anthony Alexander, who created a frame for these words with his amazing graphic design work.

If I remembered what writing was really like, I would never promise another book to a publisher. When a project is finished I tend to remember the good times, but that is not the whole story. My thanks to my family and friends for listening to me whine during the hard times and helping me to have the courage to continue to write my way towards the end of this book. I would especially like to thank my husband, partner, and friend Stewart Duncan. And also Caren Cameron and Kathleen Gregory, who stuck with me as friends, teachers, and telephone buddies throughout the three years I spent writing and researching this book.

Appendix

Building Inukshuks: Learning by Ourselves and with Others

Learning to make assessment work is an ongoing task for us as teachers. Keeping ourselves learning and on track can be a challenge in our busy lives. One approach teachers find helpful is to be part of a group of people learning together. There are many names for this. I like to call it a learning circle. I learn from the people I talk with, and they learn from me.

When we learn together, we share experiences that help us understand our thinking. This helps us grow and learn at our own pace. Sometimes a group provides the support we need to take risks. Other times it prevents us from leaping without a parachute.

Your Learning Circle

You probably already belong to a learning circle. We are learning when we talk with others about what we are trying, when we share books that are helping us learn, and when we call someone to share a success or get advice. We know that sometimes we need to learn by ourselves and sometimes we need to learn with others. Sometimes other people help us realize what we know and what we want to learn more about.

Learning circles cannot be mandated. They arise out of common interests and a willingness to extend friendship to others. They last as long as they work, coming in and out of existence as people form questions and answer them. They are circles of friends or soon-to-be friends learning together.

Teachers as Learners and Researchers

To work, learning circles must be implemented in ways that are respectful of teachers as learners. When participants are invited to be involved and when they choose what and how they are going to learn, the power of their learning can be astonishing.

- be respectful of each other

- agree that being a professional means adapting, not adopting, new ideas

- agree that there are lots of right ways to teach, assess, and learn

- ask thoughtful questions

- welcome all points of view

- limit the frequency and length of meetings

- agree how participants will take turns talking

- agree to give each speaker undivided attention without interrupting

- agree to refrain from giving advice or ideas unless the speaker requests them

- agree that conversations at the meeting should not be repeated elsewhere unless permission is granted by the person sharing the story

When potential participants choose not to accept the invitation to be involved in learning about and researching classroom assessment, get curious. It is important to trust learners—perhaps they need to learn about something else before they will be ready. They may have helpful suggestions to improve the process you are suggesting. A different process might support learning and involvement for more people.

We need to remember that we all learn in different ways and at different times. When we treat our colleagues with as much respect as we try to treat children, and when we provide a variety of learning experiences, we begin to build a safe learning environment. Ask them what kind of support they need to meet their professional goals. Unless adults feel safe enough to take the risks necessary to learn, change will never happen. Go slowly. An Inukshuk is built one rock at a time.

Guidelines to Consider

Here are some guidelines that might help you form a learning circle.

Start Small

Start with a few people you think might be interested in learning more about supporting student learning through assessment. Draw up a list of people and call them to arrange a time to get together for a first gathering. If you can only find one other person, that is fine. As time passes, you will find other kindred spirits to join you.

Your learning circle can begin by sharing favourite assessment resources or by having participants tell their own stories. Invite participants to describe incidents that caused them to become interested in improving classroom assessment for their students. Listen to each other and ask questions. Find out if there are common threads of experience. Look for possible common interests within the field of classroom assessment.

Get Organized Together

Acting as the leader of the business part of the first gathering, explain your vision for the group. Briefly touch on the following issues:

- why you want to start a group
- what the group might do or accomplish
- whether it will be more like a book club, a time to share successful classroom assessment ideas, or a combination of both
- whether or not you are going to use a book (this one or another) as a study guide
- where and how often the group might meet
- how each gathering could proceed and be organized

After you share your ideas, ask participants to share theirs. Feel your way, through conversation, toward a final agreement on these issues. Avoid being overly ambitious. The more obligations you put on yourselves, the more likely they will not be fulfilled. Consider meeting once a month rather than biweekly. Consider skipping particularly busy months.

Share Responsibility

Each meeting should be conducted by someone who's been designated in advance. This might be the group leader, the person hosting the meeting, or a volunteer. The organizer needs to make sure everyone is reminded about the upcoming meeting and must be prepared to devise alternative plans if something needs to be rearranged. Someone will also need to agree to keep the meeting on track by ensuring that everyone has a chance to contribute and that an agreed-upon structure is followed.

Works Cited

Barlow, M., and H. Robertson. 1994. *Class Warfare.* Toronto, Ont.: KeyPorter Books.

Bibby, R.W., and D.C. Posterski. 1992. *Teen Trends: A Nation in Motion.* Toronto, Ont.: Stoddart Press.

Biddle, B., and D. Berliner. 1998. *The Manufactured Crisis.* Don Mills, Ont.: Addison-Wesley Publishing Company, Inc.

Black, P., and D. Wiliam. 1998. Assessment and classroom learning. *Assessment in Education* 5, no. 1: 7-75.

Brown, J., and E. Langer. 1990. Mindfulness and intelligence: A comparison. *Educational Psychologist* 25, nos. 3-4:305-335.

Butler, R. 1987. Task-involving and ego-involving properties of evaluation: Effects of different feedback conditions on motivational perceptions, interest and performance. *Journal of Educational Psychology* 79, no. 4:474-482.

Butler, R. 1988. Enhancing and undermining intrinsic motivation: The effects of task-involving and ego-involving evaluation on interest and performance. *British Journal of Educational Psychology* 58:1-14.

Butler, R., and M. Nisan. 1986. Effects of no feedback, task-related comments and grades on intrinsic motivation and performance. *Journal of Educational Psychology* 78, no. 3:210-216.

Butterworth, R.W., and W.B. Michael. 1975. The relationship of reading achievement, school attitude, and self responsibility behaviors of sixth grade pupils to comparative and individuated reporting systems: Implication of improvement of validity of the evaluation and pupil performance. *Educational and Psychological Measurement* 35:987-991.

Calkins, L. 1991. *Living Between the Lines.* Portsmouth, N.H.: Heinemann.

Cameron, C., B. Tate, D. MacNaughton, and C. Politano. 1997. *Recognition Without Rewards.* Winnipeg, Man.: Peguis Publishers.

Cameron, C. 1999. Slowing down to the speed of learning. *Primary Leadership* 1, no. 2:61-63.

Cohen, S.A. 1988. *Tests: Marked for Life*. New York: Scholastic Bright Ideas.

Costa, A., and B. Kallick. 1995. *Assessment in the Learning Organization*. Alexandria, Va.: ASCD.

Curwin, R. 1978. The grades of wrath: Some alternatives. *Learning* 6, no. 6 (February): 60-64.

Daggart, W. 1991. Keynote address given at Ministry of Education Conference at the Victoria Conference Centre, Fall, in Victoria, B.C.

Davies, A., C. Cameron, C. Politano, and K. Gregory. 1992. *Together Is Better: Collaborative Assessment, Evaluation, and Reporting*. Winnipeg, Man.: Peguis Publishers.

DeCharms, R. 1968. *Personal Causation: The Internal Affective Determinants of Behavior*. New York: Academic Press.

DeCharms, R. 1972. Personal causation training in schools. *Journal of Applied Social Psychology* 2:95-113.

Deci, E., and R.M. Ryan. 1985. *Intrinsic Motivation and Self-Determination in Human Behavior*. New York: Plenum Press.

Deci, E., E.R. Vallerand, L.G. Pelletier, and R.M. Ryan. 1991. Motivation and education: The self-determination perspective. *Educational Psychologist* 26, nos. 3-4 (Summer-Fall): 325-346.

Dewey, J. 1933. *How We Think: A Restatement of the Relation of Reflective Thinking To the Educative Process*. Lexington, Mass.: Heath.

Dixon, N., A. Davies, and C. Politano. 1996. *Learning with Readers Theatre*. Winnipeg, Man.: Peguis Publishers.

Drummond, M.J. 1994. *Learning to See: Assessment Through Observation*. Markham, Ont.: Pembroke Publishers.

Elbow, P. 1986. *Embracing Contraries: Explorations in Learning and Teaching*. New York: Oxford University Press.

Gardner, H. 1984. *Frames of Mind: The Theory of Multiple Intelligences*. New York: Basic Books.

Gibbs C., and G. Stobart. 1993. *Assessment: A Teacher's Guide to the Issues*. 2d ed. Hodder and Stoughton.

Goleman, D. 1995. *Emotional Intelligence*. New York: Bantam Books.

Gregory, K., C. Cameron, and A. Davies. 1997. *Knowing What Counts: Setting and Using Criteria*. Merville, B.C.: Connections Publishing.

Gregory, K., C. Cameron, and A. Davies. 2000. *Knowing What Counts: Self-Assessment and Goal-Setting*. Merville, B.C.: Connections Publishing.

Gregory, K., C. Cameron, and A. Davies. In Press. *Knowing What Counts: Conferencing and Reporting.* Merville, B.C.: Connections Publishing.

Harter, S. 1978. Pleasure derived from challenge and the effects of receiving grades on children's difficulty level choices. *Child Development* 49, no. 3 (September):788-799.

Hillocks, G. 1986. *Research on Written Composition.* Champaign, Ill.: NCTE.

Hurford, S. 1998. I can see clearly now—student learning profiles. *Primary Leadership* l, no. 2:22-29.

Jensen, E. 1998. *Teaching with the Brain in Mind.* Alexandria, Va.: ASCD.

Jovanovic, L. 1979. J.H. Sissons Staff Meeting, August, in Yellowknife, N.W.T.

Kohn, A. 1993. *Punished by Rewards: The Trouble With Gold Stars, Incentive Plans, A's, Praise, And Other Bribes.* New York: Houghton Mifflin.

Kohn, A. 1999. *The Schools Our Children Deserve.* Boston: Houghton Mifflin.

Kovalik, S. 1994. *ITI The Model.* Kent, Wash.: Kovalik and Associates.

Langer, E.J. 1997. *The Power of Mindful Learning.* Reading, Mass.: Addison-Wesley Publishing Company Inc.

Le Doux, J. 1996. *The Emotional Brain.* New York: Simon and Schuster.

Lepper, M.R., and D. Greene. 1974. Turning play into work: Effects of adult surveillance and extrinsic rewards on children's intrinsic motivation. *Journal of Personality and Social Psychology* 45, no. 4 (December): 1141-1145.

Lepper, M.R., and D. Greene. eds. 1978. *The Hidden Costs Of Rewards: New Perspectives On The Psychology Of Human Motivation.* Hillsdale, N.J.: Lawrence Erlbaum.

Lincoln, Y., and E. Guba. 1984. *Naturalistic Inquiry.* Beverly Hills, Calif.: Sage Publications.

Maehr, M. 1974. *Sociocultural Origins of Achievement.* Monterey, Calif.: Brooks/Cole.

Mager, R.F., and J. McCann. 1963. *Learner Controlled Instruction.* Palo Alto, Calif.: Varian Press.

Mahoney, M.J. 1974. *Cognition and Behavior Modification.* Cambridge, Mass.: Ballinger.

Natriello, G. 1984. Problems in the evaluation of students and student disengagement from secondary schools. *Journal of Research and Development in Education* 17, no. 4:14-24.

Nye, K. 1999. Open House: Let the kids do it. *Primary Leadership* 2, no. 1:26-27.

Pinker, S. 1997. *How the Mind Works.* New York: HarperCollins Publisher.

Politano, C., and A. Davies. 1994. *Multi-Age and More.* Winnipeg, Man.: Peguis Publishers.

Politano, C., and J. Paquin. 2000. *Brain-based Learning with Class.* Winnipeg, Man.: Peguis Publishers.

Preece, A. 1995. Involving students in self-evaluation. In *Assessment in the Learning Organization,* by A. Costa and B. Kallick. Alexandria, Va.: ASCD.

Purkey, W., and J. Novak. 1984. *Inviting School Success.* Belmont, Calif.: Wadsworth.

Restak, R. 1988. *The Mind.* New York: Bantam Books.

Restak, R. 1991. *A Mind of their Own.* New York: Bantam Books.

Rothman, R. 1995. *Measuring Up: Standards, Assessment, and School Reform.* San Francisco: Jossey-Bass Publishers.

Schmoker, M. 1996. *Results: The Key to Continuous School Improvement.* Alexandria, Va.: ASCD.

Schon, D.A. 1983. *The Reflective Practitioner.* New York: Basic Books.

Schon, D.A. 1990. *Educating the Reflective Practitioner.* San Francisco: Jossey-Bass Publishers.

Seagoe, M.V. 1970. *The Learning Process And School Practice.* Scranton, Pa.: Chandler Publishing Company.

Shepard, L.A., and M.L. Smith. 1987. What doesn't work: Explaining policies of retention in the early grades. *Kappan* 69 (October): 129-134.

Shepard, L. A., and M. L. Smith. 1986. *Flunking Grades: Research and Policies on Retention.* New York: The Falmer Press.

Smith, A., and A. Davies. 1996. *Wordsmithing: A Spelling Program for Grades 3-8.* Winnipeg, Man.: Peguis Publishers.

Smith, F. 1986. *Insult to Intelligence: The Bureaucratic Invasion of Our Classrooms.* Portsmouth, N.H.: Heinemann.

Smith, F. 1991. *To Think.* New York: Columbia University, Teachers College Press.

Sprenger, M. 1998. Memory is a two way street. *Educational Leadership* 56, no. 3 (November): 65-67.

Sternberg, R. 1996. *Successful Intelligence: How Practical and Creative Intelligence Determines Success in Life.* New York: Simon and Schuster.

Stiggins, R. 1997. *Student-Centered Classroom Assessment.* 2d ed. Columbus, Ohio: Merrill Publishing.

Sutton, R. 1997. *The Learning School.* Salford, England: Sutton Publications.

Sylwester, R. 1995. *A Celebration of Neurons: An Educator's Guide to the Brain.* Alexandria, Va.: ASCD.

Tuckman, B.W. 1988. *Testing for Teachers.* 2d ed. New York: Harcourt Brace Jovanovich Publishers.

Tyler, R. 1949. *Basic Principles of Curriculum and Instruction.* Chicago: University of Chicago Press.

Walters, J., S. Seidel, and H. Gardner. 1994. Children as Reflective Practitioners. In *Creating Powerful Thinking in Teachers and Students,* by K.C. Block and J.N. Magnieri. eds. New York: Harcourt Brace.

Wiggins, G. 1993. *Assessing Student Performance: Exploring the Purpose and Limits of Testing.* San Francisco, Calif.: Jossey-Bass Publishers.

Wiggins, G. 1998. Keynote address given at Assessment Conference, October, in Augusta, Maine.

Wolf, D. 1989. Portfolio assessment: Sampling student work. *Educational Leadership* 46, no. 7 (April): 35-37.

Wolf, D. 1987. Opening up assessment. *Educational Leadership* 46:35-39.

Young, E. 2000. Enhancing student writing by teaching self-assessment strategies that incorporate the criteria of good writers. Submitted in partial fulfillment of requirements for the degree of Doctor of Education to the Department of Educational Psychology, State University of New Jersey, Graduate School of Education, Rutgers.

Zessoules, R., and H. Gardner. 1991. Authentic assessment: Beyond the buzzword and into the classroom. In *Expanding Student Assessment,* by Vito Perrone. ed. Alexandria, Va.: ASCD.

From Connections Publishing

The following related titles are also available from Connections Publishing:

Knowing What Counts 1: Setting and Using Criteria	ISBN 0-9682160-1-3
Knowing What Counts 2: Self-Assessment and Goal-Setting	ISBN 0-9682160-2-1
Knowing What Counts 3: Conferencing and Reporting	ISBN 0-9682160-3-X
Learning with Readers Theatre	ISBN 1-895411-80-7
Making Themes Work	ISBN 1-895411-60-2
Multi-Age and More	ISBN 1-895411-65-3
Recognition Without Rewards	ISBN 1-895411-89-0
Student-Involved Parent Conferences (Video)	
Together is Better: Collaborative Assessment, Evaluation, and Reporting	ISBN 1-895411-54-8
Wordsmithing: A Spelling Program for Grades 3–8	ISBN 1-895411-85-8

Ordering Options

Phone: Toll-free 1 800 603 9888
or 1 250 337 5534

Fax: 1 250 337 8113

E-mail: classscon@mars.ark.com

Post: Connections Publishing
P.O. 488
Merville, BC, V0R 2M0, Canada

Discounts available on bulk orders.